The Son of God

MARTIN HENGEL

The Son of God

*The Origin of Christology and the
History of Jewish-Hellenistic Religion*

———

FORTRESS PRESS
PHILADELPHIA

Translated by John Bowden from the German
*Der Sohn Gottes, Die Enstehung der Christologie
und die jüdisch-hellenistische Religionsgeschichte,*
published 1975 by J. C. B. Mohr (Paul Siebeck), Tübingen

First American Edition by
Fortress Press 1976

Library of Congress Catalog Card Number 75-37151
ISBN 0-8006-1227-2

Printed in Great Britain   1-1227

Contents

To Eberhard Jüngel on his Swabian coming of age

(As is well known, Swabians do not come of age until that
time when life is said to begin – at forty)

Preface

This study is based on my inaugural lecture at Tübingen on 16 May 1973. Despite necessary expansions I have deliberately kept to the structure and argument of the lecture.

The work as a whole is meant to be a contribution to the critical discussion of New Testament christology, which today has become a notable battleground. I am concerned to demonstrate that historical scholarship and theological – one might even say dogmatic – questions must not stand in unresolved contradiction to each other. On the contrary, the historian misunderstands the nature of New Testament christology unless he grasps its theological concern and its inner consistency, while a dogmatic approach which does not take seriously the historical course of christology during the first decades of primitive Christianity is in danger of becoming no more than abstract speculation. At a time when historical positivism and hermeneutical interest largely go their own ways in New Testament scholarship, it is vitally important to reunite historical research and the theological search for truth.

I am grateful to Fräulein Cordelia Kopsch for typing the manuscript, to Dr Andreas Nissen for his supervision of it and to Herr Helmut Kienle for his careful reading of the proofs.

Tübingen,   MARTIN HENGEL
New Year 1975

Abbreviations

AAG	Abhandlungen der Akademie der Wissenschaften in Göttingen
AAMz	Abhandlungen der Akademie der Wissenschaften in Mainz
AGAJU	Arbeiten zur Geschichte des antiken Judentums und des Urchristentums, Leiden
AGSU	Arbeiten zur Geschichte des Spätjudentums und Urchristentums, Leiden
AJT	*American Journal of Theology*, Chicago
ALGHJ	Arbeiten zur Literatur und Geschichte des hellenistischen Judentums, Leiden
AnalBibl	Analecta Biblica, Rome
AOAT	Alter Orient und Altes Testament, Kevelaer
ATANT	Abhandlungen zur Theologie des Alten und Neuen Testaments, Zürich
BBB	Bonner biblische Beiträge, Bonn
BEvTh	Beiträge zur evangelischen Theologie
BGBE	Beiträge zur Geschichte biblischen Exegese, Tübingen
Bibl	*Biblica*, Rome
BWANT	Beiträge zur Wissenschaft vom Alten und Neuen Testament, Stuttgart
BZNW	Beihefte zur Zeitschrift für die neutestamentliche Wissenschaft, Berlin
CH	Corpus Hermeticum
CIL	Corpus inscriptionum Latinarum, Berlin
CRAI	Comptes rendus des séances de l'académie des inscriptions et belles lettres, Paris
CSEL	Corpus scriptorum ecclesiasticorum Latinorum, Vienna

EKK	Evangelisch-katholischer Kommentar zum Neuen Testament, Neukirchen
ÉPROER	Études préliminaires aux religions orientales dans l'empire romain, Leiden
ET	English translation
ÉtBibl	Études bibliques, Paris
EvTh	*Evangelische Theologie*, Munich
FRLANT	Forschungen zur Religion und Literatur des Alten und Neuen Testaments, Göttingen
GCS	Griechischen christlichen Schriftsteller der ersten Jahrhunderte, Berlin
HAT	Handbuch zum Alten Testament, Tübingen
HNT	Handbuch zum Neuen Testament, Tübingen
HTK	Herders theologischer Kommentar zum Neuen Testament, Freiburg im Breisgau
HTR	*Harvard Theological Review*, Cambridge, Mass.
HUCA	*Hebrew Union College Annual*, Cincinnati
JAOS	*Journal of the American Oriental Society*, Baltimore
JbAC	*Jahrbuch für Antike und Christentum*, Münster
JBL	*Journal of Biblical Literature*, Philadelphia
JJS	*Journal of Jewish Studies*, London
JSJ	*Journal of the Study of Judaism in the Persian, Hellenistic and Roman Period*, Leiden
KEK	Kritisch-exegetischer Kommentar über das Neue Testament, Göttingen (Meyer Kommentar)
MPT	*Monatsschrift für Pastoraltheologie*, Göttingen
NF (NS)	Neue Folge (New Series)
NT	*Novum Testamentum*, Leiden
NTA	Neutestamentliche Abhandlungen
NTS	*New Testament Studies*, Cambridge
OTS	*Oudtestamentische Studien*, Leiden
PSI	Pubblicazioni della Società Italiana, Papiri Greci et Latini, Rome
PW	*Paulys Realencyclopädie der classischen Altertumswissenschaft*, Stuttgart
PW, 2R	Second Series, R to Z
RAC	*Reallexikon für Antike und Christentum*, Stuttgart

RB	*Revue biblique*, Paris
RÉG	*Revue des études grecques*, Paris
RGG	*Die Religion in Geschichte und Gegenwart*, Tübingen
RhMus	*Rheinisches Museum für Philologie*, Bonn
RSR	*Revue des Sciences Religieuses*
RVV	Religionsgeschichtliche Versuche und Vorarbeiten, Giessen
SANT	Studien zum Alten und Neuen Testament, Munich
SBT	Studies in Biblical Theology, London and Naperville, Illinois
SNT	Studien zum Neuen Testament, Gütersloh
SNTS	Studiorum Novi Testamenti Societas
SupplNT	Supplements to *Novum Testamentum*
SUNT	Studien zur Umwelt des Neuen Testaments, Göttingen
SVF	Stoicorum veterum fragmenta, Berlin
SVT	Supplements to *Vetus Testamentum*, Leiden
Syll.	W. Dittenberger, *Sylloge Inscriptionum Graecarum*, Leipzig
TDNT	G. Kittel and G. Friedrich, *Theological Dictionary of the New Testament*, Grand Rapids, Michigan
THAT	E. Jenni and C. Westermann, *Theologisches Handwörterbuch zum Alten Testament*, Munich
ThB	Theologisches Bücherei, Munich
TLZ	*Theologische Literaturzeitung*, Leipzig
TQ	*Theologische Quartalschrift*, Tübingen
TU	Texte und Untersuchungen zur Geschichte der altchristlichen Literatur, Berlin
TZ	*Theologische Zeitschrift*, Basle
UNT	Untersuchungen zum Neuen Testament, Leipzig
VigChr	*Vigiliae Christianae*, Amsterdam
VT	*Vetus Testamentum*, Leiden
WF	Westfälische Forschungen, Münster
WMANT	Wissenschaftliche Monographien zum Alten und Neuen Testament, Neukirchen
WUNT	Wissenschaftliche Untersuchungen zum Neuen Testament, Tübingen

ZDPV   *Zeitschrift des deutschen Palästina-Vereins,* Wiesbaden

ZNW   *Zeitschrift für die neutestamentliche Wissenschaft,* Berlin

ZPapEp *Zeitschrift für Papyrologie und Epigraphik,* Bonn

ZTK   *Zeitschrift für Theologie und Kirche,* Tübingen

I

The Problem

At the feast of the Passover in the year 30, in Jerusalem, a Galilean Jew was nailed to the cross for claiming to be Messiah. About twenty-five years later, the former Pharisee Paul quotes a hymn about this crucified man in a letter which he writes to one of the communities of the messianic sect which he has founded in the Roman colony of Philippi:

> He was in the form of God,
> (but) did not count equality with God a thing to be grasped,
> but emptied himself,
> taking the form of a slave,
> being born in the likeness of man and found in human form.
> He humbled himself
> and became obedient unto death,
> even death on a cross (Phil. 2.6–8).

The discrepancy between the shameful death of a Jewish state criminal and the confession that depicts this executed man as a pre-existent divine figure who becomes man and humbles himself to a slave's death is, as far as I can see, without analogy in the ancient world. It also illuminates the riddle of the origin of the christology of the early church.[1] Paul founded the community in Philippi in

---

[1] Cf. M. Dibelius, *RGG*[2] 1, 1593, on the 'main problem of christology'. This is the question 'how the knowledge of the historical figure of Jesus changed so quickly into belief in the heavenly Son of God'. From the abundant literature on the Philippians hymn see J. Gnilka, *Der Philipperbrief*, HTK X, 3, 1968, 111–47; R. P. Martin, *Carmen Christi, Phil. II, 5–11 in Recent Interpretation* . . ., SNTS Monograph Series 4, 1967, with an extensive bibliography; C.-H. Hunzinger, 'Zur Struktur der Christus-Hymnen in Phil. 2 und 1 Petrus 3', in *Der Ruf Jesu und die Antwort der Gemeinde, Festschrift für J. Jeremias*, 1970, 145–56; K. Wengst, *Christologische Formeln und Lieder des Urchristentums*, SNT 7, 1972, 144ff.; cf. C. Talbert, *JBL* 86, 1967, 141ff.; J. A. Sanders, *JBL* 88, 1969, 279ff.;

about the year AD 49, and in the letter which he wrote to the believers there about six or seven years later he will have presented the same Christ as in the preaching which brought the community into being. This means that the 'apotheosis of the crucified Jesus' must already have taken place in the forties, and one is tempted to say *that more happened in this period of less than two decades than in the whole of the next seven centuries, up to the time when the doctrine of the early church was completed.* Indeed, one might even ask whether the formation of doctrine in the early church was essentially more than a consistent development and completion of what had already been unfolded in the primal event of the first two decades, but in the language and thought-forms of Greek, which was its necessary setting.[2]

J. T. Sanders, *The New Testament Christological Hymns*, SNTS Monograph Series 15, 1971, 9ff., 58ff. For special problems see J. G. Gibbs, *NT* 12, 1970, 270ff.; P. Grelot, *Bibl* 53, 1972, 495ff.; 54, 1973, 25ff., 169ff., who conjectures an origin from a bilingual milieu; J. Carmignac, *NTS* 18, 1971/72, 131ff.; C. Spicq, *RB* 80, 1973, 37ff. I must refrain from going further into the most recent and utterly reckless interpretation by H.-W. Bartsch, 'Die konkrete Wahrheit und die Lüge der Spekulation', *Theologie und Wirklichkeit* 1, 1974, in which the pre-existence of Christ in the hymn is denied and the statements in the first part are related solely to the man Jesus. This is no realization of historical truth, but a triumph of ideologically motivated and utterly fantastic speculation. Bartsch's study makes it clear what New Testament exegesis can expect if it follows the newest political and theological fashions. See now O. Hofius, *Sklave und Herr*, WUNT 17, 1976.

[2] For the chronology see W. G. Kümmel, *Introduction to the New Testament*, [2]1975, 252ff., 322ff.: founding of the community 48/49; p. 332: composition of the letter either between 53 and 55 in Ephesus or between 56 and 58 in Caesarea. J. Gnilka, *Der Philipperbrief*, 1968, 3f., 24, suggests that the year 50 is 'extremely probably' the year in which the community was founded and that part A of the letter was written from Ephesus in the years 55 and 56. One or two years' difference is of little account here. The new publication of the Gallio inscription by A. Plassart, *Fouilles de Delphes Tome III, Epigraphie, Fascicule IV, Nos 276 à 350*, 1970, No 286, pp. 26ff., seems to me rather to suggest an early date; cf. id., *REG* 80, 1967, 372–8, and J. H. Olivier, *Hesperia* 40, 1971, 239f. For the whole question see my study 'Christologie und neutestamentliche Chronologie', in *Neues Testament und Geschichte, Festschrift für O. Cullmann zum 70. Geburtstag*, 1972, 43–67.

2

Criticism

This, of course, is the point at which modern criticism begins. No less a scholar than Adolf von Harnack lamented the development 'as the history of the suppression of the historical Christ by the preexistent Christ (the real Christ by the fictitious Christ) in dogmatics'. For 'this apparent enrichment of Christ amounted to an impoverishment, because it in fact obliterated the complete human personality of Christ'.[3] While he celebrated Paul as the founder of 'western and Christian civilization' in *What is Christianity?*,[4] he also saw a danger that 'under the influence of the Messianic dogmas, and led by the impression which Christ made, Paul became the author of the speculative idea that not only was God in Christ, but that Christ himself was possessed of a peculiar nature of a heavenly kind . . . Christ's *appearance* in itself, the entrance of a divine being into the world, came of necessity to rank as the chief fact, as itself the real redemption.' Of course that was not yet the case with Paul, since for him the cross and resurrection were the crucial facts and the incarnation could be interpreted in moral terms as 'an example for us to follow' (II Cor. 8.9). But the incarnation 'could not permanently occupy the second place; it was too large'. However, 'when moved into the first place it threatened the very existence of the Gospel, by drawing away men's thoughts and interests in another direction. When we look at the history of dogma, who can deny that this was what happened?'[5] But this

[3] A. von Harnack, *Lehrbuch der Dogmengeschichte* (unaltered reprint of fourth edition of 1909), 1964, I, 704f.
[4] A. von Harnack, *What is Christianity?*, 1901 reprinted 1957, 179.
[5] Harnack, op. cit., 185; cf. the reference to the 'dangers' of Pauline christology, among which he includes the doctrines of 'objective redemption', 183. On this see K. Barth/E. Thurneysen, *Briefwechsel, Vol. II, 1921–1930*, 1974, 36, 'as a result of which the two others (C. Stange and

means the dogmatic ossification of faith: 'The living faith seems to be transformed into a creed to be believed; devotion to Christ, into Christology.'[6] Thus Harnack's critical observations, which may be regarded as characteristic of the christological thought of wider circles of modern Protestantism. In contrast to 'speculative progress' there was a demand for a 'return' to the simple gospel of Jesus,[7] unburdened by christological speculation, since – to use Harnack's words once more: 'The Gospel, as Jesus proclaimed it, has to do with the Father only and not with the Son.'[8]

Jewish scholars made the same kind of criticism. The Galilean was rediscovered in modern Jewish scholarship and attempts were made to 'bring him home' to Judaism. Apostasy from the faith of the fathers began, rather, with Paul. As an example we may take the picture of Paul drawn by the Erlangen philosopher of religion, H. J. Schoeps: 'It was Paul who for the first time, reflecting on the messianic figure (of Jesus), made out of a title of dignity an ontological affirmation and raised it to a mythical level of thought.'[9] His 'Christ has become a supernatural being and approximates to

---

E. Hirsch) once again suspect that I have a "physical doctrine of redemption", which in this generation is about the worst thing that you can say about anyone'.

[6] Harnack, op. cit., 193.

[7] Cf. Harnack, *Lehrbuch der Dogmengeschichte*, 704f., and *What is Christianity?*, 184: 'The formation of a correct theory of and about Christ threatens to assume the position of chief importance, and to pervert the majesty and simplicity of the Gospel' (the author puts this sentence in italics). Harnack does not remember here that Pauline christology is chronologically earlier than the synoptic gospels in their 'simplicity'. Perhaps the 'original gospel', too, was not as 'simple' as Harnack would have liked. Did not Jesus' own proclamation of the coming Son of Man as judge of the world contain a quite 'speculative', apocalyptic messianology? Might not the first 'speculative' fall of early Christian theology be already connected with this heavenly figure? It is understandable – at least on apologetic grounds – that some of the most recent exegesis wants to purge the original proclamation of Jesus of these apocalyptic shadows. That will make it more modern, but not more authentic.

[8] A. von Harnack, *What is Christianity?*, 144 (the author puts this sentence in italics).

[9] H. J. Schoeps, *Paul: The Theology of the Apostle in the Light of Jewish History*, 1961, 150 (here as elsewhere the translation has been slightly altered in the cause of accuracy).

gnostic heavenly beings ... This heavenly Christ seems to have
wholly absorbed the earthly Jesus into himself ... The myth
clearly represented here ... points to pagan spheres',[10] more
specifically to the 'religious syncretism of Asia Minor'.[11] Schoeps'
verdict is consistent and clear: 'Hence we see in the υἱὸς θεοῦ
belief the sole, albeit decisive heathen premiss of Pauline thought.
All that belongs to and flows from it ... is un-Jewish and akin to
heathen ideas of the time.'[12] When Pauline christology and soteriology combined with this 'un-Jewish belief in the Son of God' and
became 'the dogma of the Christian church, it burst the framework
of Jewish belief once and for all'. Schoeps concludes with a reference to Harnack's verdict: 'The "acute Hellenization of Christianity", so much discussed in its day, takes place at this point.'[13]
It would be fascinating to trace further this *encounter between*

[10] Schoeps, op. cit., 153.
[11] Schoeps, op. cit., 158. In this connection Schoeps refers to the old
hypothesis of influence from Sandan, the city-god of Tarsus, who in the
Hellenistic period was worshipped as Heracles. For criticism see the
excellent review by A. D. Nock, *Gnomon* 33, 1961, 583, n. 10 = *Essays on
Religion and the Ancient World*, 1972, II, 930. The hypothesis that Sandan-
Heracles was a dying and rising god is extremely questionable, see also
H. Goldman, *JAOS* 60, 1940, 544ff., and *Hesperia* Suppl. 8, 1949, 164ff.
Zwicker, 'Sandon', *PW*, 2R, I, 2, 1920, 2267, was already stressing 'our
scanty knowledge of the nature of Sandan', which '(leads) to various uncertain interpretations'. Quite apart from this, according to Acts 22.3;
26.4; Phil. 3.5; Gal. 1.13f., we must take into account the possibility that
Paul moved to Jerusalem at a very early age, as a child, and was brought
up there. See W. C. van Unnik, *Sparsa Collecta* I, 1973, 259–327.
[12] Schoeps, op. cit., 158 (italicized by the author, though this is not
indicated in the English translation).
[13] Schoeps, op. cit., 167. Cf. what he already wrote in *Aus frühchrist-
licher Zeit*, 1950, 229: 'In my view, no analogous speculations are capable
of demonstrating that belief in the υἱὸς θεοῦ, alien to the Jewish-
Christian primitive community, is Jewish.' As will be demonstrated, this
argument is erroneous. Schoeps here begins from a normative concept of
'Judaism' which only developed out of Pharisaism in the post-Christian
period in the constant controversy with Christianity, cf. G. Lindeskog,
Die Jesusfrage im neuzeitlichen Judentum, 1938, 15. He completely fails to
notice the phenomenon of *Jewish mysticism*, and like many Jewish his-
torians suppresses it for apologetic reasons (see pp. 89f., n. 150 below). The
article cited by Schoeps, A. Marmorstein, 'The Unity of God in Rabbinic
Literature', in *Studies in Jewish Theology*, 1950, 101ff., cf. 93ff., does
reflect this later controversy between Judaism and Christianity.

reformed Judaism and liberal Protestantism in their criticism of christological dogma,[14] but the responsible theologian, historian and exegete can no longer be satisfied with D. F. Strauss's much-repeated remark: 'The true criticism of dogma is its history.' He must attempt, rather, not only to analyse the historical derivation of the conceptions and terms created by early Christian belief but also to understand them and interpret them theologically.[15] This task always includes a critical examination of earlier criticism.

[14] The controversy over Paul runs parallel to the 'restoration of Jesus to Judaism'; cf. already the two works by Joseph Klausner, *Jesus of Nazareth*, 1925, and *From Jesus to Paul*, 1944, or the more recent studies by Schalom Ben-Chorin, *Bruder Jesus*, [3]1970, and *Paulus*, 1970; cf. also L. Baeck, 'Romantische Religion' (1922), in *Aus drei Jahrtausenden*, 1958, 47ff., and more positively 'The Faith of Paul', *JJS* 3, 1952, 93–110, and M. Buber, *Two Types of Faith*, 1951, 79ff. See R. Mayer, 'Christentum und Judentum in der Schau Leo Baecks', *Studia Delitzschiana* 6, 1961, 58–64. In contrast to the books from Klausner to Schoeps, the simple booklet by Ben-Chorin, while preserving a Jewish standpoint, shows the most thorough understanding of Paul and recognizes above all the Jewish roots of Pauline thought: 'By way of a generalization one can say that, consciously or unconsciously, Paul took over the building material for his theological construction from Judaism. In this powerful edifice of Pauline theology there is hardly an element which is not Jewish. Sometimes it seems as if something quite different, new and strange, were appearing,but on closer inspection the Jewish background to Paul's thought appears, even where he seems to be in abrupt contrast to Judaism' (p. 181).

[15] K. Barth/E. Thurneysen, *Briefwechsel* (n. 5 above), 253f., on the doctrine of the Trinity in the early church: 'Men and brethren, what a mess! But don't think that it is all old rubbish; in the right light everything seems to make sense . . .'

3

The Testimony of Paul

Let us begin with *the earliest* primitive Christian *evidence that we have*, the authentic letters of Paul. Statistical evidence alone seems to contradict Schoeps' view that the title Son of God is of central significance for Paul. For Paul uses the two titles 'Lord' and 'Son of God', which describe Jesus in a special way as an exalted, heavenly figure, quite disproportionately. Whereas he uses '*Kyrios*' 184 times, we only find '*huios theou*' 15 times. The distribution of the two terms is also striking. 'Son of God' appears most frequently in the letters where the controversy with the Jewish tradition is at its height, in Romans and Galatians (7 and 4 times respectively), whereas the two letters addressed to the community in Corinth, which was now really threatened with 'acute Hellenization', contain 'Son of God' only 3 times. There was a danger there, in true Greek fashion, that the new message would be interpreted, not in gnostic terms, but – following a false interpretation of Paul's doctrine of freedom – as a doctrine of salvation along the lines of the cult of Dionysus and the mysteries.

Kramer, who has made the most recent analysis of the christological titles in Paul, comes to a quite different result from Schoeps on the basis of the 'statistical' evidence and form-critical analyses:

1. 'In Paul's view both the title Son of God and the ideas associated with it are of relatively minor importance.'

2. Paul usually employs the term in stereotyped formulas which he has taken over from earlier tradition, and 'the original meaning of the title has already faded'.[16]

Now this means that the alleged lapse into the speculative Hellenization of christology must already have taken place in the early church before the time of Paul!

[16] W. Kramer, *Christ, Lord, Son of God*, SBT 50, 1966, 189, 186.

Before we turn to the difficult question of the historical derivation of the title Son of God, we must therefore examine Kramer's
two arguments. Let us first turn to the significance of the title in
Paul.[17] This significance could depend not only on statistics, but
also on the context of the use of the title within Paul's letters. It is
striking that the title appears 3 times right at the beginning of
Romans, in the introduction, and that Paul uses it to describe the
content of his gospel (1.3, 4, 9). It occurs 3 times again at the
climax of the letter, in ch. 8, the point of which could be summed
up in a single sentence: The 'Son of God' makes us 'sons of God',
who are to participate in his heavenly *doxa* (8.3, 29, 32).[18] This
indicates that for Paul the *soteriological* rather than the speculative
significance of the term stands in the foreground. Galatians makes
the same impression. Here Son of God appears at the beginning
of the letter in connection with the radical change in the apostle's
way of life:

> But when he (God) who had set me apart before I was born, and had
> called me through his grace, was pleased to reveal his Son to me, in
> order that I might preach him among the Gentiles . . . (1.15f.).

Here Paul shows at the same time that Son of God is the real
content of his gospel.[19] We find the title also – just as in Rom. 8 – at
the climax of the letter:

---

[17] For what follows see E. Schweizer, υἱὸς θεοῦ, *TDNT* 8, 1972, 382ff.;
J. Blank, *Paulus und Jesus*, SANT 18, 1968, 249–303; W. Thüsing, *Per
Christum in Deum*, NTA NF 1, ²1969, 144–7.

[18] Above all Rom. 8.29f.; cf. Phil. 3.21. See J. Blank, op. cit., 287ff.;
H. R. Balz, *Heilsvertrauen und Welterfahrung*, BEvTh 59, 1971, 109ff.
For criticism of Kramer see 110, n. 246: he has 'made the framework
of the statements about the Son taken over by Paul too narrow'. Cf. also
W. Thüsing, op. cit., 121ff., and P. Siber, *Mit Christus leben*, ATANT 61,
1971, 152ff. Paul's terminology here is strongly moulded by tradition.

[19] J. Blank, op. cit., 222ff.: 'The "subject matter" of the revelation is
the "Son of God", Jesus Christ who is risen from the dead' (229, cf. 249,
255). Similarly H. Schlier, *Der Brief an die Galater*, KEK, ¹²1962, 55:
'The revelation of God to Paul has a personal object: God reveals to him
his Son. Here that means the exalted Lord.' P. Stuhlmacher, *Das paulinische Evangelium I. Vorgeschichte*, FRLANT 95, 1968, 81f., defines the
revelation of the Son as 'allowing the Risen One to be seen enthroned by
God and thus as the Son of God who is appointed ruler', cf. id., *ZTK* 67,
1970, 30. This could be a reference to the early confession of the Son of

But when the time had fully come, God sent forth his Son, born of woman, born under the law, to redeem those who were under the law, so that we might receive adoption as sons (Gal. 4.4f.).[20]

The point is again clearly soteriological: the 'Son of God' frees us to become 'sons of God'.

This finding is confirmed by a quite different text at the beginning of II Corinthians:

As surely as God is faithful, our word to you has not been Yes and No. For the Son of God, Jesus Christ, whom we preached among you . . . was not Yes and No; but in him it is always Yes (1.18f.).

Here too the content of the apostle's message is the Son of God. As Bachmann already observed in his commentary, the solemn use of the title 'Son' emphasizes that 'the Son belongs together with the Father'. In his incarnation, God's Yes is clearly spoken to abandoned man: 'For all the promises of God find their Yes in him' (1.20). And because through the Son, God's Yes has become reality for all men, the community can conclude and endorse its prayer to the glory of God 'through him' with the 'Yes' of the Amen.

In I Corinthians, too, the Son first appears at the beginning of the letter (1.9) and then again at a climax (I Cor. 15.28). At the end of all things, when even the last power, death, has been conquered by the parousia of Christ and the general resurrection, '*the Son* himself will also be subjected to him who put all things under him, that God may be everything to everyone'.[21] Thus Paul uses

---

God in Rom. 1.3f. For the dative understanding of *en emoi* see F. Mussner, *Der Galaterbrief*, HTK IX, 1974, 86f., n. 45.

[20] Cf. E. Schweizer, *TDNT* 8, 383f.; J. Blank, op. cit., 260–78; W. Thüsing, op. cit., 116f.; G. Eichholz, *Die Theologie des Paulus im Umriss*, 1972, 157ff.; F. Mussner, op. cit., 268ff.: 'The Son's destiny had a definite saving purpose' (270); 273: 'The Son is wholly Son for us.' Paul does not introduce the 'Son christology for speculative reasons . . . but out of soteriological concern'.

[21] For the history of the interpretation of this passage, which was so significant for the christology of the early church, see now E. Schendel, 'Herrschaft und Unterwerfung Christi. I Kor. 15, 24–28', in *Exegese und Theologie der Väter bis zum Ausgang des 4. Jhdts*, BGBE 12, 1971.

the term Son to describe as the content of his mission preaching
not only the pre-existent and incarnate redeemer of the world, but
also the perfecter of creation and history. He does the same thing
in his earliest writing, I Thess. 1.10, which speaks of the expectation of the Son coming from heaven, 'who delivers us from the
wrath to come'.[22]

It is also striking that in almost all his statements about the
Son of God, Paul uses the title *when he is speaking of the close bond
between Jesus Christ and God, that is, of his function as the mediator
of salvation* between God and man. We must therefore support the
old master of the history of religions school, W. Bousset, against
Kramer when he observes that while 'Son of God' – like the verb
'believe' – appears much more rarely in Paul than in the Johannine
literature, we do find it 'at the climactic points of the presentation'.
Here Bousset can even appeal to Luke: 'The only place where the
author of the book of Acts uses the title ὁ υἱὸς τοῦ θεοῦ occurs
in the summary of the Pauline preaching' (9.20).[23]

While we can follow Bousset and the history of religions school,
and also Harnack and Schoeps, in their stress on the significance of
the title 'Son' for Paul, Bousset's hypothesis that 'we have to do
with an independent creation of Paul'[24] is less convincing. Form-
critical and traditio-critical analysis has long shown that Paul took
over this title from earlier tradition. That is clear simply from the
fact that he connects it with the event of his call, which will have
taken place between AD 32 and 34.[25] In particular, there are two
formulations which the apostle could have taken over from the
church which came before him (or, more precisely, existed alongside him, presumably in Syria):

1. *The sending of the pre-existent Son into the world.* Here we

---

[22] Cf. G. Friedrich, *TZ* 21, 1965, 512ff., and E. Schweizer, *TDNT* 8,
371, 383, who refer to Rev. 2.18 and suggest that 'Son of God' here has
been introduced into a saying about the Son of Man. The only question
is where and when this substitution took place.

[23] W. Bousset, *Kyrios Christos*, ET 1970, 206. For criticism of Kramer's
theory see also J. Blank, op. cit., 283f.; cf. 300ff.

[24] W. Bousset, op. cit., 207.

[25] M. Hengel, 'Christologie und neutestamentliche Chronologie' (n. 2
above), 44, 61f. Here, too, the difference of a year or two is immaterial.

find the same syntactical pattern in Rom. 8.3 and Gal. 4.4: God is the subject, followed by a verb of sending as predicate. The object is the Son, followed by a final clause introduced by ἵνα, which explains the soteriological significance of the sending. We often find this statement formulated in the same way – independently of Pauline tradition – in the Johannine writings (John 3.17; I John 4.9, 10, 14). On the other hand, the theological interpretation is typically Pauline: liberation from the power of sin and the law and the appointment of the believer to the relationship of being a son of God himself.[26]

2. *The giving up of the Son to death*. The apostle begins the radiant conclusion of Rom. 8.32ff.:

If God is for us, who is against us? He who did not spare his own Son but gave him up for us all, will he not also give us all things with him?

Here we have on the one hand echoes of the Old Testament account of Isaac's sacrifice,[27] and in addition what is presumably once again an established pattern which has also been written down in a well-known verse of the Gospel of John:

[26] W. Kramer, op. cit., 111ff.; E. Schweizer, 'Zum religionsgeschichtlichen Hintergrund der "Sendungsformel", Gal 4.4f., Rö 8.3f., Joh 3.16f., 1 Joh 4.9', *ZNW* 57, 1966, 199–210 = *Beiträge zur Theologie des Neuen Testaments*, Zürich 1970, 83–95; id., *TDNT* 8, 374ff., 386; id., *Jesus*, 1971, 81ff. The objections to the existence of a 'sending formula' made by K. Wengst, *Christologische Formeln und Lieder des Urchristentums*, SNT 7, 1972, 59, n. 22, do not convince me. Even if we heed H. von Campenhausen's warning, *ZNW* 63, 1972, 231, n. 124, that we should be sparing with the use of the term 'formula', so that the 'voracious formula-hydra' does not grow 'more rampant heads', the usage seems to me to be legitimate. So too F. Mussner, *Galater*, 271ff.: 'a pre-Pauline pattern of proclamation ... filled with a variety of material' (272).

[27] ὅς γε τοῦ ἰδίου υἱοῦ οὐκ ἐφείσατο, cf. Gen. 22.12, 16: καὶ οὐκ ἐφείσω τοῦ υἱοῦ σου τοῦ ἀγαπητοῦ δι' ἐμέ. Cf. further Ps.Philo 18.5; 32.2ff. Literature in Blank, op. cit., 294ff., and E. Käsemann, *An die Römer*, HNT 8a, 1973, 237. For the Jewish parallels and their relationship to Rom. 8.32 see G. Vermes, *Scripture and Tradition in Judaism*, ²1973, 193–227 (218ff.); S. Spiegel, *The Last Trial. On the Legends and Lore of the Command to Abraham to offer Isaac as a Sacrifice: The Akedah*, New York 1969, 82ff. See there, 83, n. 26, the anti-Christian polemic of R. Abin in the name of R. Hilkiah, Agg. Ber. c. 31, ed. Buber, 64.

God so loved the world that he gave his only-begotten Son . . . (3.16).

In Gal. 2.20 Paul no longer speaks of God, but of the Son as the subject of this action:

> The life I now live in the flesh I live by faith in the Son of God, who loved me and gave himself for me.

Here the title Son describes the uniqueness of the saving event, the magnitude of the sacrifice for our sake. Here again we have Johnnine parallels, though they do not use the title Son (10.11; 15.13; I John 3.16).[28] These formal statements about the Son of God, which therefore probably already existed in Paul's time, have two complementary focal points:

1. The sending of the pre-existent Son into the world.
2. His being given up to death on the cross.

The two themes recur in the Philippians hymn quoted at the beginning of this study, where the divine being of the pre-existent Christ and the slave's death of the incarnate Jesus are connected. The difference is that the title 'Son of God' does not appear there. Rather, in the final act of exaltation the crucified one is acclaimed as 'Kyrios', an indication of the close relationship in content between the titles 'Kyrios' and 'Son of God'.[29]

We must also look at Colossians, the authenticity of which is disputed. Here we find hymnic expressions where the subject is again the 'beloved Son' (1.13):

> He is the image of the invisible God, the first-born of all creation; for in him all things were created. . . . (1.15).

Even here the reference to death on the cross cannot be absent at the end (1.20). Here, however, it is not a self-emptying as in Philippians, but the work of an all-embracing reconciliation of the

[28] For the formulas of Rom. 8.32 and Gal. 2.20 see W. Kramer, op. cit., 116ff.; cf. also the criticism by W. Popkes, *Christus Traditus*, ATANT 49, 1967, 201ff., though in my view it does not meet the point; also E. Schweizer, *TDNT* 8, 384; J. Blank, op. cit., 298ff., and F. Mussner, *Galater*, 50f., 183, n. 77.

[29] We should not therefore assume two fundamentally different historical roots for them. Rather, they will both come from the same religious milieu.

world.[30] We will not go more closely into the many problems of the hymn at this point, as it seems to have a clearly post-Pauline character.[31] We shall keep to those features which we find again in Paul himself. First mention must be given to the *mediation* of Christ *at creation*. Paul alludes to it in a passage which seems like a formula:

> For us there is one God, the Father, from whom are all things and for whom we exist, and one Lord, Jesus Christ, through whom are all things and through whom we exist (I Cor. 8.6).

The Father is the primal ground and goal of creation, whereas Christ is the mediator.[32] At the same time, we can also see here the

[30] For more recent literature see W. Pöhlmann, *ZNW* 64, 1973, 53, n. 2: the various hypotheses do not lead to the construction of any original form that is at all certain. This is also true for the statement about atonement in 1.20b, which cannot definitely be shown to be an addition. At any rate, the hymn was Christian from the beginning. Pöhlmann gives a considered attempt at a reconstruction on p. 56. For the reconciling of the world cf. E. Schweizer, *Beiträge zur Theologie des Neuen Testaments*, 1970, 132ff., 139ff. For the parallel in Eph. 2.14–18 see P. Stuhlmacher in *Neues Testament und Kirche, Festschrift R. Schnackenburg*, 1974, 337–58.

[31] With E. Lohse, *Colossians and Philemon*, Hermeneia, 1971, 41ff., against W. G. Kümmel, *Introduction to the New Testament*, ²1975, 342ff. Colossians and Ephesians are, however, substantially earlier than the Pastoral Epistles. I do not think it impossible that they were written before AD 70.

[32] P. H. Langkammer, *NTS* 17, 1970/71, 193ff.: 'It cannot be doubted that there are the beginnings of a Son of God theology here' (194). This formula which Paul directs against the multiplicity of pagan gods and lords will have had predecessors in the theology of the Jewish mission, cf. e.g. Sib. 3.11; Fr. 1.7 (Geffcken, 227); also Fr. 3.3 (230); 3.629, 718; II Macc. 7.37; Dan. 3.45; Josephus, *Antt.* 4, 201, etc., cf. M. Hengel, *Die Zeloten*, AGSU 1, 1961, 101ff. The acclamatory form may correspond to the formula ᶜΕΙΣ ΘΕΟΣ in pagan cults, although these formulas are almost always later, see E. Peterson, ᶜΕΙΣ ΘΕΟΣ, FRLANT 41, 1926, 227ff., 253ff., 276ff., 304ff. At any rate, the connection with the idea of creation indicates a Jewish origin, cf. Aristeas 132. On the other hand, it is too fanciful to relate it to the fragmentary Orphic-Dionysic Gurob papyrus from the third century BC, as does K. Wengst, *Christologische Formeln und Lieder des Urchristentums*, SNT 7, 1972, 139. The riddle of this papyrus and the formula εἷς Διόνυσος which appears in it, in an obscure context, for the first time, is still unsolved, see M. P. Nilsson, *Geschichte der griechischen Religion*, ²1961, II, 244f., and O. Schütz, *RhMus* 87, 1938, 241ff., who attempts a very hypothetical reconstruction

close connection between the titles 'Lord' and 'Son of God'. The fact that we have only this one statement about Christ's mediation in creation – almost, one might say, by chance – merely shows how little we know of the whole of Paul's theology. We only know the tip of the iceberg, fascinating though that may be.

There remains the question why Paul could use the title 'Kyrios' so much more frequently than 'Son of God', although the content of the two titles is closely connected and they are in part interchangeable, because they both refer to the risen and exalted Christ. While the much rarer 'Son of God' above all expressed the unique relationship of the exalted Christ to God, the Father, the title Kyrios, which could also be used as a form of address in prayer and in acclamation, expressed above all the relation between the exalted Christ and his community, or the individual believer. The formula *Kyrios Iesous* (Rom. 10.9; I Cor. 12.3; Phil. 2.11) made up the basic confession, reduced to its briefest form, by the community of the crucified and risen Jesus, who had been exalted by God and would come again. Thus Kyrios became the current title in worship and in the individual life of the believer, while *the form 'Son of God', with its more complicated language, was kept for exceptional usage, at the climax of certain theological statements*.

In Paul Christ is also the *eikon*, the '*image of God*', whose radiance shines out in the proclamation of the gospel (II Cor. 4.4). In this concept the idea of the mediator of revelation and that of the mediator at creation are combined. The εἰκὼν θεοῦ has connections with the μορφή θεοῦ of the Philippians hymn; indeed, one might ask whether the one term does not interpret the other.[33]

---

of the damaged papyrus. εἰς Διόνυσος here is not an acclamation (246, line 23). For Christ as mediator at creation see H. F. Weiss, *Untersuchungen zur Kosmologie des hellenistischen und palästinischen Judentums*, TU 97, 1966, 288, 301, 305ff.; H. Hegermann, *Die Vorstellung vom Schöpfungsmittler im hellenistischen Judentum und Urchristentum*, TU 82, 1961, 88f., on Col. 1.15ff., and 111f., 135, 137, 200.

[33] F.-W. Eltester, *Eikon im Neuen Testament*, BZNW 23, 1958, 133; R. P. Martin, *An Early Christian Confession: Philippians II.5–11 in Recent Interpretation*, 1960; see also id., *Carmen Christi. Philippians II.5–11 in Recent Interpretation and in the Setting of Early Christian Worship*, 1967, 107ff. However, the two terms should not be over-hastily identified with each other, see already J. Behm, μορφή, *TDNT* 4,

This designation, too, is concerned with the soteriological significance of Christ. In him, God's image – with E. Jüngel one might
even say God's 'parable' – God's real being, his love, is made
visible for believers (I John 4.8f.).

Paul's conception of the Son of God, which was certainly not his
own creation but goes back to earlier community tradition before
Paul's letters, thus proves to be quite unique. Jesus, the recently
crucified Jew, whose physical brother James – the ἀδελφὸς τοῦ
κυρίου – Paul himself had personally known well (Gal. 1.19; 2.9;
cf. I Cor. 9.5), is not only the Messiah whom God has raised from
the dead, but much more. He is identical with a divine being,
before all time, mediator between God and his creatures. That is,
at the same time he is mediator of God's saving revelation which,
for example, accompanied Israel through the wilderness as a water-
bearing rock (I Cor. 10.4). Born as man, he took the Jewish law
upon him and died the most shameful death known to antiquity,
death on a cross.

1967, 752, and more recently, with numerous linguistic examples, C.
Spicq, *RB* 80, 1973, 37–45. Cf. Sib. 3,8: ἄνθρωποι θεόπλαστον ἔχοντες ἐν
εἰκόνι μορφήν; CH 1, 12: περικαλλὴς γάρ, τὴν τοῦ πατρὸς εἰκόνα ἔχων· ὄντως
γὰρ καὶ ὁ θεὸς ἠράσθη τῆς ἰδίας μορφῆς.

4

The Theory of the
History of Religions School

It is quite understandable that this new picture of Christ should be claimed to represent a *new 'Hellenistic Christianity'*.[34] R. Bultmann, who here emerges as to some extent the spokesman of the history of religions school, could describe it as 'basically a wholly new religion, in contrast to the original Palestinian Christianity'. Speculation of this kind must have seemed even further removed from the proclamation of Jesus as Bultmann described it, following Wellhausen: 'pure Judaism, pure prophetic teaching',[35] thus completing the return of Jesus to Judaism. At the same time the great Marburg scholar corrected Harnack's thesis of a 'Hellenizing of Christianity' along the lines of the history of religions school. He argued that the cause of this new form was not – as was still supposed in the nineteenth century, under the influence of F. C.

[34] W. Heitmüller, *ZNW* 13, 1912, 320–37 = K. H. Rengstorf (ed.), *Das Paulusbild in der neueren deutschen Forschung*, WF XXIV, 1964, 124–43; cf. also the Bonn dissertation by H. W. Boers, *The Diversity of New Testament Christological Concepts and the Confession of Faith*, 1962, 114ff., and M. Hengel, 'Christologie und neutestamentliche Chronologie' (n. 2 above), 47ff.

[35] R. Bultmann, *Faith and Understanding*, 1969, 271, 283. For Jesus see also id., *Jesus and the Word*, ²1958, 48f., and *Theology of the New Testament*, I, 1952, 27, for the phrase 'prophet and rabbi'; see M. Hengel, *Nachfolge und Charisma*, BZNW 34, 1968, 46ff. See already J. Wellhausen, *Einleitung in die drei ersten Evangelien*, 1905, 113: 'Jesus was not a Christian, but a Jew. He did not proclaim a new faith but taught men to do the will of God.' On this see the controversy between R. Bultmann, 'The Primitive Christian Kerygma and the Historical Jesus', in Carl E. Braaten and Roy A. Harrisville (eds.), *The Historical Jesus and the Kerygmatic Christ*, 1964, 15–42, and E. Käsemann, *Essays on New Testament Themes*, SBT 41, 1964, 37; id., *New Testament Questions of Today*, 1969, 42f.

Baur – a speculative philosophical interest on the part of Greek
Gentile Christians, but a new 'cultic piety',[36] moulded by the
mystery religions. In his criticism of the christological confession
of the World Council of Churches in 1950, Bultmann made this
theory of the history of religions school more precise in connection
with the 'Son of God':

> For the figure of a son-deity suffering and dying and raised again to
> life is also known to the mystery religions, and gnosticism above all
> is aware of the notion of the Son of God become man – of the
> heavenly redeemer become man.[37]

Bultmann, his teachers Bousset and Heitmüller, and his followers
repeated this argument *ad nauseam* without verifying it adequately
by the ancient sources. If they were right, then a few years after
the death of Jesus an 'acute Hellenization', or more precisely *a
syncretistic paganization of primitive Christianity*, must have come
about among the spiritual leaders of Jewish Christianity like
Barnabas, or the former scribe and Pharisee Paul. Moreover, this
must have taken place either in Palestine itself or in neighbouring
Syria, say in Damascus or Antioch. In that case, the criticism of
Paul's christology by the Jewish philosopher of religion H. J.
Schoeps would be quite justified. It is clear that such an extra-
ordinary historical development would have been in radical and
irreconcilable contradiction to the preaching of Jesus. In that case
a decision would have to be made between Jesus and Paul.

In what follows, we shall attempt to illuminate the development
of the title Son of God, moving back from Paul to the origins of
Christian belief. In so doing, we shall consider whether there really
was a fundamental breach in many respects in the rise of christology between Jesus and Paul, or whether it is not the case that – at
least after the death of Jesus or the Easter event – it is possible to
see an inner trend in christological thought which contradicts

[36] R. Bultmann, *Faith and Understanding*, 271f.
[37] R. Bultmann, *Essays*, 1955, 279. But see the embittered and at the
same time knowledgeable protest against the speculative theories of the
history of religions school in K. Holl, 'Urchristentum und Religionsgeschichte', *Gesammelte Aufsätze zur Kirchengeschichte* II, 1928, 1–32,
esp. pp. 18ff. on Paul.

Herbert Braun's theory and shows that christology was not a random 'variable' but *the consistent 'constant'*.[38]

[38] H. Braun, *Gesammelte Studien zum Neuen Testament und seiner Umwelt*, ²1967, 272. Cf. the early protest by E. Käsemann, *New Testament Questions of Today*, 1969, 37f.

5

The Meaning of 'Son of God' and the History of Religions

We must first – within the limits imposed here – attempt to discover the philological and religious significance of the term 'Son of God' in Semitic and in Greek contexts.[39] The meaning of the Greek '*huios*' is almost completely limited to physical descent, and a transferred meaning is only marginal. Its usage is further limited by the fact that it is often replaced by the 'more comprehensive expression' *pais* or *paides*, small boy, children.[40]

I. *The Old Testament*

The Hebrew '*ben*' (Aramaic *bar*) is very different: 'It is the most common term of relation in the OT (some 4850 instances).'[41] In contrast to '*huios*' it not only (or even primarily) designates physical descent and relationship, but is a widespread expression of subordination, which could describe younger companions, pupils and members of a group, membership of a people or a profession, or a characteristic. In this extended sense it was also used in a number of ways in the Old Testament to *express belonging to God*. First of all were the *members of the heavenly court*, the angels, who are often

[39] For what follows see W. von Martitz/G. Fohrer, υἱός, *TDNT* 8, 1969, 335ff., 340ff. On the other hand, the study by Petr Pokorný, *Der Gottessohn*, Theologische Studien 109, 1971, a preliminary to an article in *RAC*, is of little help. For the Old Testament see also J. Kühlewein in E. Jenni/C. Westermann, *THAT* 1, 1971, 316–25; W. Schlisske, *Gottessöhne und Gottessohn im AT*, BWANT 97, 1973.

[40] W. von Martitz, *TDNT* 8, 335f.

[41] G. Fohrer, *TDNT* 8, 340.

called 'sons of the gods' in the Old Testament. These may originally have been depotentiated gods of the Canaanite pantheon, but
this can no longer be detected in the Old Testament texts: as
Yahweh's creatures they are quite subordinate to him.[42] In Daniel,
which is near to the New Testament period, Nebuchadnezzar sees
a fourth figure 'whose appearance is like a son of the gods' in the
fire alongside the three Jewish confessors (3.25).[43] After Hippolytus this passage was interpreted by the church fathers with
reference to Christ,[44] while a rabbi in the fourth century, in anti-
Christian terms, affirmed that for this blasphemy God had delivered the king over to an angel of Satan who began to smite him
because in fact only 'his angel' was written there.[45]

God's people, Israel, is addressed in a special way as 'sons' or
even 'son of God', because it has been chosen by God and is the
object of his care and love: 'And you shall say to Pharaoh, "Thus
says Yahweh, Israel is my first-born son, and I say to you, 'Let
my son go that he may serve me'; and if you refuse . . . I will slay
your first-born son" ' (Exod. 4.22f.).[46] Finally, *the Davidic king*
could also be called 'son of God', following Egyptian models. This
expressed the divine legitimation of the ruler. The interpretation
of the relationship of God and king as that of father and son already
appears in the oracle of Nathan, II Sam. 7.12–14; it is taken up

[42] G. Fohrer, *TDNT* 8, 347ff.: Gen. 6.2, 4; Job 1.6; 38.7; 2.1; Pss. 29.1;
89.7, cf. Ps. 82.6 and Deut. 32.8f. (LXX and 4QDeut^q). Cf. also W.
Schlisske, op. cit., 15ff.: the Canaanite-Ugaritic parallels are the most
interesting.

[43] *dāmeh l^{e}bar-'^{e}lāhin*. Theodotion: ὁμοία υἱῷ θεοῦ. LXX: ὁμοίωμα
ἀγγέλου θεοῦ. The statement is in remarkable contrast to 7.13: *k^{e}bar
'^{e}nāš*.

[44] A. Bentzen, *Daniel*, HAT I, 19, ²1952, 37.

[45] Ex. R. 20.10 after R. Barachiah, c. AD 340, see Billerbeck I, 139.
There are further examples of rabbinical polemic against the use of the
designation 'Son of God' for angels in P. S. Alexander, 'The Targumim
and Early Exegesis of the "Sons of God" in Genesis 6', *JJS* 23, 1972,
60–71. R. Simeon b. Johai cursed all those who called the angels 'sons of
God': Gen. R. 26.5 (see ibid., 61).

[46] Cf. Jer. 31.9, 20; Hos. 11.1. God as father of Israel: Deut. 32.6, 18;
Jer. 3.4; all Israel as sons (and daughters) of Yahweh: Deut. 14.1; 32.5,
19; Isa. 43.6; 45.11; Hos. 2.1 etc.; see G. Fohrer, op. cit., 351ff.; W.
Schlisske, op. cit., 116–72.

and developed in Ps. 89.4ff. and I Chron. 17.13; 22.10 and 28.6.[47]
Isa. 9.5 also belongs in this context. Ps. 2.7: 'He (Yahweh) said to
me, "You are my son, today I have begotten you" ', probably also
comes from the Jewish royal ritual. Scholars have rightly stressed
that the 'today' excludes all physical concepts of begetting.[48] More
precisely, H. Gese has stressed that 'you are my son' represents a
realized promise of salvation which is further strengthened by the
addition of the clause 'today I have begotten you'. 'That the house
of David are sons of God is not foreign mythology, but the conception of the relationship with the *naḥᵃlā*-lord to be found in
Israelite family law.' 'According to Ps. 2.7 and 110.3 . . . the
enthronement of the Davidic king on Zion is understood as birth
and creation through God.'[49] The juridical concepts of adoption
and legitimation are hardly adequate to describe this happening
appropriately. It is certainly no coincidence that Psalms 2 and 110
become the most important pillars of the early church's christological argument from scripture.

II.   *Greek and Hellenistic parallels*

The possibilities of developing the Old Testament statements
about the Son of God thus appear to be remarkably varied. This

[47] For the Egyptian and Near Eastern background see H. Brunner, *Die
Geburt des Gottkönigs*, 1964; K. H. Bernhardt, *Das Problem der altorienta-
lischen Königsideologie im AT*, SVT 8, 1961; G. W. Ahlström, *Psalm 89.
Eine Liturgie aus dem Ritual des leidenden Königs*, Lund 1959, 111f.; see
182ff. for II Sam. 7.14ff.; id., *VT* 11, 1961, 113ff.; H. Gese, 'Der Davids-
bund und die Zionserwählung', *ZTK* 61, 1964, 10–26 = *Vom Sinai zum
Zion*, BEvTh 64, 1974, 113–29; K. Seybold, *Das davidische Königtum im
Zeugnis der Propheten*, FRLANT 107, 1972, 26ff.; W. Schlisske, op. cit.,
78–115.

[48] G. Fohrer, op. cit., 351: an Egyptian ritual underlies that at Jerusalem. 'The Egyptian idea of physical sonship is changed into a legal one.'
The question is whether the bare alternative 'physical or legal' really does
justice to the act of election and new creation.

[49] 'Natus ex virgine', in *Probleme biblischer Theologie. Gerhard von Rad
zum 70. Geburtstag*, 1971, 82 = *Vom Sinai zum Zion*, 139. For Ps. 110.3,
see p. 81 (= *Sinai zum Zion*, 138): the text probably meant originally:
'On the holy mountain from your mother's womb, from the dawn of the
morning I bore you.' The 'holy mountain' corresponds to Zion, the 'dawn of
the new day is the pendant to the "today" of Ps. 2.7'. Cf. W. Schlisske, 100ff.

cannot so readily be said of the alleged Greek and Hellenistic parallels. Certainly the prolific *Zeus*, πατὴρ ἀνδρῶν τε θεῶν τε,⁵⁰ produced countless divine, semi-divine and mortal offspring, but there is no link between these παῖδες Διός of Hellenic nature religion and the early Christian confession of the *one* Son of the *one* God. And those who in enlightened fashion followed the Stoics in confessing that all men are by nature children of Zeus because they bear his seed in them by virtue of their reason, no longer need a 'son of God' as mediator and redeemer. Here the motto could only be: 'Become what you already are!'⁵¹ When Luke makes Paul quote the famous verse of Aratus, 'We are his offspring', in the Areopagus speech (Acts 17.28),⁵² he does so with bewildering inconsistency.

⁵⁰ *Iliad* 1, 544; *Odyssey* 1, 28; 20, 201, etc. We find πατήρ about 100 times out of the 300 or so passages in Homer where Zeus has an epithet: see M. P. Nilsson, 'Vater Zeus', in *Opuscula selecta*, 2, 710ff.: id., *Geschichte der griechischen Religion*, I, ³1967, 336f. See G. M. Calhoun, 'Zeus the Father in Homer', *Transactions and Proceedings of the American Philological Association* 66, 1935, 1–12.

⁵¹ W. von Martitz, *TDNT* 8, 337: Chrysippus and Cleanthes already suggest divine sonship, but it appears in so many words in Epictetus: *Diss.* I, 3, 2; 13, 3; 19, 9; II, 16, 44 (Heracles) cf. 8, 11; III, 22, 82; 24, 15f. The use of 'Son of God' in the Christian-Pythagorean *Sentences of Sextus* has probably also been influenced by Stoicism: see H. Chadwick, *The Sentences of Sextus*, Cambridge 1959, nos. 58, 60, 135, 221 (Lat.), 376b: the wise man is 'God's son' and therefore 'godlike' (18f., 45, 48–50, 381, see p. 106). Cf. G. Delling, 'Zur Hellenisierung des Christentums in den "Sprüchen des Sextus" ', in *Studien zum NT und zur Patristik. E. Klostermann zum 90. Geburtstag dargebracht*, TU 77, 1961, 208–41, esp. 210f. There is also strong stress on kinship with God, indeed divine sonship, in the Olympian speech of Dio Chrysostom of Prusa (*Or.* 12.27–34, 42, 61, etc.). M. Pohlenz, *Stoa und Stoiker*, 1950, 341f., 382, conjectures dependence on Posidonius. Cf. above all Dio Chrysostom 12.28 with Acts 17.27 and on it K. Reinhardt, *PW* XXII, 1, 1953, 812f. In the discourse 'On the Law', the law is said to be 'of insuperable . . . might' with an allusion to Heracles – ὁ τοῦ Διὸς ὄντως υἱός (ch. 8).

⁵² The Aratus quotation already appears in the earliest Jewish 'philosopher of religion' whom we can discover, Aristobulus, about the middle of the second century BC, see M. Hengel, *Judaism and Hellenism*, I, 1974, 165, from Eusebius, *PE* 13, 12, 5f.

ぬ155
II.(a)   Mysteries, dying and rising sons of God
and the ruler cult

The constantly repeated view that the development of the Son of God christology is a typically Hellenistic phenomenon and represents a break in primitive Christianity hardly bears closer examination. The Hellenistic mysteries did not know of sons of God who died and rose again, nor did the mystic himself become a child of the god of the mysteries.[53] Dying vegetation deities like Phoenician Adonis, Phrygian Attis or Egyptian Osiris had no function as sons of God. In late antiquity they were often regarded as men from the mythical primal period, to whom – as to Heracles – immortality was given after their death. Of all the 'sons of Zeus' in Greek religion, *Heracles* might be most likely to provide analogies to christological ideas, but he never became a god of the mysteries: he only had a strong influence as a model for the ruler cult, i.e. on political religion, and on the religious views of popular philosophy. Even where, as e.g. in Ps-Seneca's Heracles dramas, he is represented as '*soter*', '*pacator orbis*' (*Her. oet.* 1990), and indeed as vanquisher of death, we in fact have no more than a poetic extension of the true, model ruler and wise man *par excellence*. He 'earned heaven by his deeds of valour', so he can ask his father for 'the world' (*Her. oet.* 97f.). His victory over death and chaos (*Her. fur.* 889ff.; *Her. oet.* 1947ff.) merely represents the victory of the Logos, divine reason, over all the powers that are hostile to reason. For this, *virtus in astra tendit, in mortem timor* (1971).[54] The Zagreus myth, in which

[53] M. P. Nilsson, *Geschichte*, II, ²1961, 688f.: 'In Christianity believers are often called children of God, but as far as I know the initiate is never called a child of the god in any of the mystery religions ... Although mythology was familiar with a large number of children of deities, expedients had to be found for making the idea of divine sonship credible in the mysteries ... The great contribution of Christianity was to understand the fatherhood of God in this sense (i.e. of trustful love), thus making man's divine sonship part of the essence of its belief.' The evidence adduced by R. Merkelbach, *ZPapEp* 11, 1973, 97, which is supposed to indicate that in the mysteries men 'experienced ... that they were truly descended from a god or from a "king" ', on the other hand, quite misses the point. E.g. Heliodorus 2, 31, 2 is merely a theme that is widespread in folk-tales and comedies.

[54] G. Wagner, *Das religonsgeschichtliche Problem von Rö 6,1–11*, ATANT

39, 1962, 180ff. on Adonis; 124ff. on Osiris, and 219ff. on Attis. Adonis was not a god of the mysteries at all, and was no more a god of salvation than Attis. Osiris and his mysteries, which are first attested by Apuleius, were quite overshadowed by those of Isis: initiation to Osiris was an appendix to initiation to Isis, in which money played more than a small part: Apuleius, *Met.* 11, 27ff.; cf. the fraud of the priests of Isis in Rome, Josephus, *Antt.*, 18, 65ff. The concept of 'dying and rising gods' is being questioned increasingly today, see C. Colpe, 'Zur mythologischen Struktur der Adonis-, Attis- und Osirisüberlieferungen', in *lišān mithurti, Festschrift für W. Freiherr von Soden*, AOAT 1, 1969, 28–33, and W. Schottroff, *ZDPV* 89, 1973, 99–104, especially 103f. For the function of Adonis, Osiris and Attis in the Hellenistic period see also A. D. Nock, *Essays on Religion and the Ancient World*, 1, 1972, 83: 'Attis, Adonis, Osiris die, are mourned for, and return to life. Yet it is nowhere said that *soteria* comes by their death.' None of the dying vegetation deities died 'for' other men, 2, 934: 'As for the "dying gods", Attis, Adonis and Osiris, it is to be remembered that, in the traditional stories, they, like most of the deities of popular religion, were deemed to have been born on this earth and to have commenced their existence at that point in time; they might descend into death, but they had not descended into life.' In other words, the decisive theme of 'sending' is absent. Pre-existence and sending are again absent with Heracles. His death and apotheosis have only limited saving significance for mankind. His apotheosis is the reward for his primal superhuman virtue. He is therefore *soter* and *euergetes* as typically understood by Hellenistic political religion from the time of Alexander, as annihilator of evil-doers and bringer of political peace. Like the Stoic wise man, the ruler must imitate him or reproduce his deeds in his own; in other words, 'in accordance with' the great exemplar he must make his salvation through his own virtue. For Epictetus, he is the symbol that all men who are endowed with reason are sons of Zeus (*Diss.* II, 16, 44; III, 24, 16, cf. also his example as son of Zeus, III,26, 31). He is regarded 'as the best of all mankind, a godlike man and rightly to be considered a god' because in utter poverty he 'ruled earth and sea', had 'self-control and hardness, he wished to be powerful, not to enjoy luxury': Ps. Lucian, *Cyn.* 13. In other words, his divinity or sonship consisted solely in the realization of his *arete* (Cornutus, 31; Max. Tyr., 15, 6, 2). In my view the orientalizing of Heracles in the dramas of Seneca by J. Kroll, *Gott und Hölle*, 1932, reprinted 1963, 339–447, goes too far. W. Grundmann, *ZNW* 38, 1939, 65ff., is quite senseless in seeking to attribute a 'Heracles christology' to the Hellenists of Acts 6.1 because of the occurrence of the terms '*Archegos*' and '*Soter*' in Acts 3.15; 4.12; 5.31. His role as a 'protective or apotropaic spirit' in ancient popular belief no more affects christology than his identification with Melkart of Tyre. At best one could indicate analogous complexes of thoughts and ideas which are generally typical of the ancient world, see e.g. C. Schneider, *Geistesgeschichte des antiken Christentums*, I, 1954, 53f., 57; H. Braun, *Gesammelte Studien*, 256ff.; M. Simon, *Hercule et le christianisme*, Paris 1955. Of course, in a

the child Dionysus is torn apart by the Titans, consumed and then reconstituted in miraculous fashion,[55] has even less to do with early Christian thought. It should also be remembered that we have more detailed accounts about the real 'oriental' mystery deities or their cults only from the second and third centuries AD. The mysteries were originally a typically Greek form of religious practice, which only had to be 'exported' to subject eastern territories in the Hellenistic period. More recent investigations of the most important oriental 'mystery religion' in the Greek-speaking East, the Isis cult, by F. Dunand, *Le culte d'Isis dans le bassin oriental de la Méditerranée* (ÉPROER 26, 1973, Vols. I–III), and L. Vidman, *Isis und Sarapis bei den Griechen und Römern* (RVV 29, 1970), say what has long been known, making it more precise by an abundance of evidence, with all the clarity that could be desired, and one can only hope that in the end it will also come to the notice of New Testament exegesis, so that the worn-out clichés which suppose crude dependence of earliest Christianity between AD 30 and AD 50 on the 'mysteries' may give way to a more pertinent and informed verdict: 'The great wave of the oriental mystery religions only begins in the time of the empire, above all in the second century, as we have stressed many times already. The struggle and at the same time the first beginnings of a synthesis of the most powerful oriental cults also begin in this century' (Vidman, 138). In the

---

structural comparison, the fundamental differences which are usually passed over in historical comparisons of religions (e.g. in the far too simple collection of quotations by Herbert Braun) would also emerge. But see E. Käsemann, *Das wandernde Gottesvolk*, FRLANT 37, 1939, 65 (against H. Windisch): 'But to use Heracles as an example or to talk of an adoptionist christology is to miss the real situation.'

[55] See W. Fauth, *PW*, 2R, IX, 2, 1967, 2221–83, cf. esp. 2279f. for alleged influence on early Christianity. The myth of Dionysus-Zagreus played a decisive role above all in dualistic Orphic speculations (cf. O. Schütz, *RhMus* 87, 1938, 251ff.); the mysteries of Dionysus at the time of the empire seem to have been less influenced by him. For the eucharist, W. Heitmüller, *RGG*[1] 1, 20f., points simultaneously to the aetiology of the Passover in Exod. 12 and the Zagreus myth, an example of the uncritical free association of the history of religions school. For the whole question see also M. P. Nilsson, op. cit., II, 364ff., and A. D. Nock, op. cit., 2, 795f.

second century AD, Christianity was already widespread and established; it was a strong competitor, but hardly the object of syncretistic alienation any longer. At this period syncretistic gnosticism was engaged in bitter struggles with Christianity. We can
hardly draw conclusions about the early period from it, and cannot
therefore simply transpose the conditions depicted by Apuleius or
even by the Christian fathers from the second century, like Justin,
Clement of Alexandria and Tertullian, to the time between AD 30
and AD 50 which is of particular interest to us. Moreover, we know
virtually nothing about the extent of the mystery cults in Syria in
the first half of the first century BC. There is no indication that they
were particularly widespread there at this early period or that they
had a strong religious influence. On the contrary, we should reckon
rather that there is strong Christian influence on the later evidence
of mysteries from the third and fourth centuries AD. Finally, we
must distinguish between the *real cults* and a widespread *'mystery
language'*. The latter certainly derives from the religious terminology of the specifically Greek mysteries of Eleusis and Dionysus,
but had long since gained complete independence. As the examples
of Artapanus, the Wisdom of Solomon and Philo show, it had also
been taken over by the synagogues of the diaspora. Evidence of it
in the New Testament still does not mean direct dependence on
the mystery cults proper. In his *Theology of the New Testament*,
Bultmann, to take one example, may postulate the dependence of
Paul on 'certain Gnostic groups organized as mystery-cults. In one
such group, for example, the mystery-god Attis had coalesced with
the Gnostic redeemer-figure.' But this is a pure figment of the
imagination which obscures, rather than illuminates, the religious
background of the early Syrian communities. On the other hand,
the Greek Corinthians do seem to have misunderstood Paul's
message in terms of the ecstatic mysteries of Dionysus, with which
they were probably familiar.[56] Furthermore, the designation υἱὸς

---

[56] Cf. Bultmann, *Theology of the New Testament*, I, 298, similarly 170f.
K. Holl, *Gesammelte Aufsätze*, II, 7, already referred to the question of
chronology: '*Certain* (author's italics) evidence for the great upsurge of
the mysteries is only available from the second century AD.' The cult of
Mithras from Ptolemaic Egypt in the third century BC which he mentions

is a survival from Persian rule and has nothing to do with the later mysteries, cf. Nilsson, op. cit., II, 36, n. 2; 669, n. 9. For the origin of the mysteries of Mithras and their treatment in Justin and Tertullian see now C. Colpe, in *Romanitas et Christianitas, Studia I. H. Waszink*, 1973, 29–43, esp. 37, n. 1. For the problem of the language of the mysteries see A. D. Nock, op. cit., 2, 796ff.: 'The terminology, as also the fact, of mystery and initiation acquired a generic quality and an almost universal appeal' (798). That is, the use of mystery language in no way signifies direct dependence on specific 'mysteries'. Even Judaism did not escape this influence, see 801ff.: Philo 'refers to pagan cult-mysteries with abhorrence but finds the philosophic metaphor of initiation congenial' (802). Similarly I, 459ff., 'The Question of Jewish Mysteries', and the discussion of Goodenough's theories which is associated with it: 'The metaphor of initiation was by its philosophic usage redeemed from any undue association with idolatry; it was particularly appropriate, inasmuch as it expressed the passive and receptive attitude of mind which Philo held to be necessary' (468). This is even more the case if one suggests that primitive Christianity or Paul are 'dependent' on the Hellenistic mysteries. In reality they are dependent on the Greek-speaking synagogue, which partly used the religious *koine* of its environment. Cf. A. D. Nock's review of Bultmann's *Primitive Christianity* in *Nuntius* 5, 1951, 35ff., and the protest there against his interpretation of the mysteries and of gnosticism. For a criticism of earlier research on the mysteries in relation to the New Testament see also H. Krämer, *Wort und Dienst, Jahrbuch der Kirchlichen Hochschule Bethel*, NF 12, 1973, 91–104. The most recent assertion by H.-W. Bartsch, 'Die konkrete Wahrheit' (n. 1 above), 120, that '*in the mystery cults, which spread out from Iran* (my italics), there opened up a possibility of overcoming humiliation in the ecstatic experience of the cult, despite the continuation of slavery', is quite unscientific, but not surprising in view of the knowledge of the Hellenistic environment to be found in German New Testament scholarship. The confusion of the mystery religions with the supposedly pre-Christian gnostic redeemer myth which becomes evident here and even more on pp. 26f. shows that the author still has not got beyond Reitzenstein's misleading theories. Even in classical times, slaves were allowed to be initiated into the earliest Greek mysteries of Eleusis, whereas the most important mysteries in Hellenistic-Roman times, those of Dionysus, were above all for the more exalted members of society. Here ecstasy traditionally played a part, but not slaves. The great inscription of Tusculum, according to which slaves were also admitted as long as they belonged to the *familia* of the noble mistress Agrippinilla is an exception. As in the time of the empire the *thiasoi* of Dionysus had largely become upper-class traditional associations (see e.g. the Io Bacchae in Athens in the second century AD, Ditt., *Syll.*³, 1109, lines 40–46), where ecstatic experience retreated into the background, this experience was sought in new cults like primitive Christianity. The nearest parallel to what went on in Corinth still seems to me to be Livy's account of the scandal of the θεοῦ, son of God, is relatively rare in the Hellenistic world and, with one exception, is never used as a title. The exception is the Greek translation of *divi filius*, son of the divinized, a title which Augustus took soon after the murder of Caesar and which is reproduced on Greek inscriptions as θεοῦ υἱός.[57] But this terminology too was no more a serious influence on the conceptuality of the earliest Christianity which was developing in Palestine and Syria than the title Kyrios used of the ruler, which had become more frequent since Claudius, or the εὐαγγέλια which appears on individual imperial inscriptions.[58] This official, secular state religion was at best a negative stimulus, not a model. The first conflicts only arose a generation or two later under Nero, in AD 64, and Domitian.

Bacchanalia in Rome in 186 BC (39, 85ff.). Pagan polemic kept transferring the charges made at that time to Christians, cf. W. Pöhlmann, *TLZ* 95, 1970, 43, certainly with no historical justification at a later date. However, there must have been points of contact in the Pauline communities which gave rise to an interpretation along the lines of the Greek *mysteries* because of their ecstatic experience of the spirit and their very lively worship. But all this still has very little to do with dualistic gnosticism; see p. 33, n. 66 below. For the whole question see F. Bömer, *Untersuchungen über die Religion der Sklaven in Griechenland und Rom*, 3: *Die wichtigsten Kulte der griechischen Welt*, AAMz 1961, 4, 351–96, and M. P. Nilsson, *The Dionysiac Mysteries of the Hellenistic and Roman Age*, 1957.

[57] A fundamental distinction must be drawn between the numerous παῖδες or υἱοὶ Διός and υἱὸς θεοῦ as a title. For this reason alone, the collection of parallels in H. Braun, *Gesammelte Studien*, 255ff., is extremely doubtful. Υἱὸς θεοῦ is *not* a widespread title in 'eastern religion', to which the 'Hellenistic community' resorted. For the ruler cult see P. Pokorný, *Der Gottessohn* (n. 39 above), 15ff.; W. von Martitz, *TDNT* 8, 336; F. Taeger, *Charisma*, 2, 1960, 98, and index, 708, s.v. 'Gotessohnidee'. For resistance from Augustus, Tiberius etc., see S. Lösch, *Deitas Jesu und antike Apotheose*, 1933, 47ff. Individual instances may be found in P. Bureth, *Les Titulatures impériales dans les papyrus, les ostraca et les inscriptions d'Égypte*, 1964, 24, 28. The title is not very frequent and rarely appears alone. After Claudius we find κύριος much more frequently. This 'son' terminology had a predecessor in the East in the designation of Ptolemaic kings as 'son of Helios' (i.e. of the sun-god Re) and of Alexander the Great as the son of Zeus Ammon.

[58] For the term εὐαγγέλιον see P. Stuhlmacher, *Das paulinische Evangelium, I. Vorgeschichte*, FRLANT 95, 1968, 196ff.

II.(b)   *Divine men*

The classical philologist Wülfing von Martitz has also shown that
the title son of God should not be over-hastily associated with the
type of the so-called θεῖος ἀνήρ, the divine man, especially as it
is questionable how far one can speak at all of this as an established
type in the first century AD. The sources to which Bieler refers in
his well-known book[59] almost all come from Neo-Platonism and
the church's hagiography.[60] Of course, from the heroes of the iron
age onwards, Greece is familiar with the physical descent of great
warriors and wise men from individual gods, and stories of miraculous births are associated with them as in the case of Pythagoras,
Plato, Alexander, Augustus and Apollonius of Tyana. However,
we do not find in this context the combination of pre-existence and
sending into the world which is typical of Pauline christology –
that is, apart from a few untypical exceptions to which we shall
return later.[61] Consequently in his much-cited but presumably

---

[59] L. Bieler, ΘΕΙΟΣ ΑΝΗΡ. *Das Bild des "göttlichen Menschen" in
Spätantike und Frühchristentum*, I/II, 1935/36 (reprinted 1967).

[60] W. von Martitz, *TDNT* 8, 337f., 339f.: θεῖος ἀνήρ is by no means
a fixed expression, at least in the pre-Christian era . . . One cannot tell
from the material even that such θεῖοι are usually sons of gods. When,
therefore, divine sonship is associated with description as θεῖος this is
quite accidental. The conceptual spheres of divine sonship and θεῖος
may well be related, but the terminology does not support this association.' For legitimate criticism of the inflationary use of θεῖος ἀνήρ in more
recent literature on the New Testament see O. Betz, 'The Concept of the
So-called "Divine Man" in Mark's Christology', in *Festschrift Allen P.
Wikgren*, SupplNT 33, 1972, 229–40; E. Schweizer, *EvTh* 33, 1973,
535ff.; J. Roloff, *TLZ* 98, 1973, 519, and for the miracle stories G.
Theissen, *Urchristliche Wundergeschichten*, SNT 8, 1974, 262ff., cf. 279ff.
The warning by K. Berger, *ZTK* 71, 1974, 6, is very appropriate: 'A
collective abstract which is inappropriate for explaining individual cases
and which should in any case only be used with the greatest care.'

[61] Even H. Braun has to concede this in his pretty row of supposed
parallels to New Testament christology, see *Gesammelte Studien*, 258f.
and n. 47. The possible variation in the different forms of divine descent
can be seen in the case of the religious founder Alexander of Abonuteichus
in the second century AD. He introduced the cult of the snake-god Glycon
as the cult of the new Asclepius, son of Apollo and grandson of Zeus,
claimed that he himself was descended from the divine miracle doctor
Podaleirus, the son of Asclepius, and that he fathered his daughter by

little-read book on 'The Son of God',[62] G. P. Wetter was essentially able to refer only to sources which had been influenced by Christianity. He refers above all to those mysterious wandering beggar-prophets whom the Platonist Celsus will have encountered on his travels in Phoenicia and Palestine in the middle of the second century AD.[63] They proclaimed: 'I am God, or a son of God (θεοῦ παῖς), or a divine spirit. And I have come. For already the world is going to ruin, and you, O men, are to perish because of (your) iniquities.' The whole context, and the introduction with the Christian triad of God, Son and Spirit, shows that in his anti-Christian pastiche Celsus is not depicting real prophets, but is parodying the Christian missionaries and their founders, to unmask them as religious frauds. And when later Christian sources claim that individual figures like Simon Magus, the author of all heresies, or the mysterious Samaritan Dositheus, gave themselves out to be sons of God, we have polemical stylizations rather than historical accounts.[64] For the same reason, the Didache can say that the Anti-Christ will appear in person as the Son of God.[65]

Selene. In other words, he made himself a great-great-grandson of Zeus. There were countless variations on the theme, but it has very little to do with 'Son of God' in christology (see Lucian, *Alex.* 11, 14, 18, 35, 39f.). He himself is said to have been a pupil of a pupil of Apollonius of Tyana and also to have understood himself to be a second Pythagoras. At the celebration of the 'torchlight mysteries' there was a representation not only of the birth of Apollo and his son Asclepius, but also of the union of the mother of Alexander with Asclepius' son Podaleirus and of the goddess Selene with the founder of the mysteries himself, as a '*hieros gamos*' (38f.). His hate was directed especially against Christians and Epicureans, both of whom he regarded as '*atheoi*' (25, 38). For the whole question see O. Weinreich, *Ausgewählte Schriften*, Vol. 1, 1969, 520–51.

[62] G. P. Wetter, *Der Sohn Gottes*, FRLANT 26, 1916.

[63] Origen, *C. Cels.* 7, 9. Cf. the 'trinity' of Simon Magus according to Hippolytus, *Phil.* 6, 19, and Irenaeus, 1, 23, 1. D. Georgi, *Die Gegner des Paulus im 2. Korintherbrief*, WMANT 11, 1964, 118ff., is one example of the uncritical interpretation of this much-cited passage. He connects it with itinerant Jewish missionaries. O. Michel, *TZ* 24, 1968, 123f., draws attention to the parallel between ἥκω δέ and the prophetic appearance of Josephus before Vespasian (*BJ* 3, 400).

[64] Simon Magus: Ps. Clem., *Hom.* 18, 6, 7; *Passio Petri et Pauli* 26 (Lipsius/Bonnet 1, 142). Dositheus: Origen, *C. Cels.* 6, 11.

[65] 16.4: καὶ τότε φανήσεται ὁ κοσμοπλανὴς ὡς υἱὸς θεοῦ καὶ ποιήσει σημεῖα καὶ τέρατα.

II.(c)   *The gnostic redeemer myth*

There remains the hypothetical *gnostic myth of the sending of the Son of God into the world*. Here we have a typical example of a modern – one might almost say pseudo-scientific – development of a myth which either leaves the foundation of historical research, the chronology of sources, out of account, or manipulates it in an arbitrary fashion. There really should be an end to presenting Manichaean texts of the third century like the 'Song of the Pearl' in the *Acts of Thomas* as evidence of supposedly pre-Christian gnosticism and dating it back to the first century BC. In reality there is no gnostic redeemer myth in the sources which can be demonstrated chronologically to be pre-Christian. This state of affairs should not be confused with the real problem of a later gnosticism standing apart from Christianity, as we find it, e.g. in the Hermetica and in some of the Nag Hammadi writings.[66]

[66] It is to the credit of C. Colpe, *Die religionsgeschichtliche Schule*, FRLANT 78, 1961, that he brought this hypothetical construction crashing down. Typical examples of unhistorical and speculative work on gnosticism are: A. Adam, *Die Psalmen des Thomas und das Perlenlied als Zeugnisse vorchristlicher Gnosis*, BZNW 24, 1959, and W. Schmithals, *Die Gnosis in Korinth*, FRLANT 66, 1956, ³1969. The latter's reaction to Colpe's work from the second edition of 1965, 32–80, onwards only shows his complete inability to learn. J.-E. Menoud, *RSR* 42, 1968, 289–325, has clearly shown that the much-cited 'Song of the Pearl' from the *Acts of Thomas* certainly cannot be used as evidence for a pre-Christian redeemer myth. The present form is a Manichaean redaction; an earlier form could go back to Syrian Christianity, under Jewish-Christian influence. At any rate, it presupposes the Christian christological tradition. For the newest, utterly fanciful work by H.-W. Bartsch on supposed pre-Christian gnosticism see above p. 1, n. 1. Cf. the posthumously published article by A. D. Nock, 'Gnosticism', *Essays*, 2, 940–59 = *HTR* 57, 1964, 255–79, which is to some extent a 'last testament'; cf. also R. Bergmeier, 'Quellen vorchristlicher Gnosis?', in *Tradition und Glaube, Festgabe für K. G. Kuhn zum 65. Geburtstag*, 1971, 200–20; cf. id., *NT* 16, 1974, 58ff. and now the thorough investigation by K. Beyschlag, 'Zur Simon-Magus-Frage', *ZTK* 68, 1971, 395–426, and id., *Simon Magus und die christliche Gnosis*, WUNT 16, 1974, who demonstrate that even the Samaritan 'magus' Simon should not be regarded as a key witness for 'pre-Christian gnosticism'. One may hope that the 'gnostic fever' (G. Friedrich, *MPT* 48, 1959, 502), which has already died down in the meantime will completely disappear and make way for a more appropriate assessment of the phenomenon. It is remarkable how much influence it still has in popular theological literature, in theological colleges and in examination work.

Gnosticism itself is first visible as a spiritual movement at the end
of the first century AD at the earliest, and only develops fully in the
second century. Neither Jewish wisdom speculation nor Qumran
and Philo should be termed 'gnostic'. As chief witness here I can
appeal to one of the most significant specialists in ancient religion,
A. D. Nock, whose clear verdict, based on the sources, is far too
little known in Germany: 'Certainly it is an unsound proceeding
to take Manichaean and other texts, full of echoes of the New
Testament, and reconstruct from them something supposedly
lying back of the New Testament.'[67] Without going further into
the much disputed question of the origin of gnosticism, I would
only say that in addition to the combination of Jewish speculation
connected with wisdom and creation, together with apocalyptic, on
the one hand and a popular dualistic Platonism on the other, early
Christianity itself was a catalyst in the rise of the gnostic systems. To
quote A. D. Nock again: 'It was the emergence of Jesus and of the
belief that he was a supernatural being who had appeared on earth
which precipitated elements previously suspended in solution.'[68]

As far as I can see, there are only very few parallels in the
Graeco-Roman world to the sending of a pre-existent divine
redeemer figure into the world, and these are remote. First of all,
of course, we must make a clear distinction between these and the
view widespread in the ancient world that all human *souls* were
sent into the world from heaven and returned there. We must also
leave out of account the fact that these souls could be said to be
godlike in some way, or to be of divine origin.[69] We are not

[67] *Essays*, 2, 958.
[68] A. D. Nock, loc. cit. For the influence of Middle Platonism on
gnosticism see H. Langerbeck, *Aufsätze zur Gnosis*, AAG, 3 F. 69, 1967,
17ff., 38ff. and H. J. Krämer, *Der Ursprung der Geistmetaphysik*, 1964,
223ff.
[69] A. D. Nock, *Essays*, 2, 935f.; cf. E. Rohde, *Psyche*, [2]1898, reprinted
1961, II, 165, n. 1; 269ff.; 304f.; 324f., n. 1. For the period up to Plato
see D. Roloff, *Gottähnlichkeit, Vergöttlichung und Erhöhung zu seligem
Leben*, 1970, 192ff.: in Empedocles; 203ff.: in Plato. The Orphic-
Pythagorean myth of the transmigration of souls favoured ideas of this
kind. The entry of the pre-existent soul into an earthly body could thus
be interpreted as a guilty fall (Empedocles), as the consequence of fatal
weakness (*Phaedrus* 246a, 6ff.), as a combination of choice and destiny
(*Republic* 617e–621b) or as divine will (*Timaeus* 41a, 7–44b, 7; 90d, 1f.).

concerned with this 'constant coming and going' of souls, which corresponds to a notion which was almost a matter of course in late antiquity and has nothing to do with gnostic speculation either, but with a unique, once-for-all happening, which is the consummation of history: 'When the time was fulfilled, God sent forth his Son.' This presupposes neither the gnostic myth, which is completely oriented towards protology, nor the timeless myth of Greek and oriental nature religion, but Jewish apocalyptic thought.

II.(d)   *The sending of the redeemer into the world and related conceptions*

We shall attempt to consider the Hellenistic 'analogies' rather more closely. Reference should first be made to the demythologizing interpretation of the doctrine of the Greek gods in the Stoic Cornutus: '*Hermes*, son of Zeus and Maia, is the Logos which the gods have sent us from heaven.' Of course this is not a sending into history, but a mythical expression for the fact that 'they created man as the only living being on earth who is endowed with reason'.

For the late Hellenistic and Roman period see A.-J. Festugière, *La Révélation d'Hermès Trismégiste*, III, *Les doctrines de l'âme*, 1953, 27ff., 63ff.; M. A. Elfrink, *La descente de l'âme d'après Macrobe*, Philosophia Antiqua 16, 1968. Numerous tomb inscriptions show that these views were popular: cf. e.g. W. Peek, *Griechische Grabgedichte*, 1960, no. 353, 2ff. (first/second century AD): '. . . But his immortal heart ascended to the blessed ones, for the soul is eternal, which gives life and came down from the godhead (καὶ θεόφιν κατέβη) . . . the body is only the garment of the soul, consider my divine part'; 465, 7ff. (second/third century AD): '. . . but the soul which came down from heaven entered the dwelling of the immortals. The corruptible body rests in the earth. But the soul which was given to me dwells in the heavenly home.' Cf. also the answer to the question 'Who are you? Where do you come from? I am a son of the earth and the starry heaven?', which appears often on the Orphic gold leaves, see Kern, *Orph. fragm.*, pp. 105ff., no. 32. The idea of the pre-existence of souls was also taken over by Judaism, Billerbeck, II, 341ff. Philo can interpret Jacob's ladder in Gen. 28.12 with the ascending and descending angels in terms of the ascent and descent of souls: *De somn.* 1, 133ff. H. Braun, *Gesammelte Studien*, 258f., nn. 46f., does not note this possibility in his parallels to 'pre-existence' or the 'descent of the divine being'.

Hermes is the *keryx* and *angelos* of the gods in so far as we know their will through the rational thoughts which are implanted in us. As the 'rational principle', of course, he has lost all personal features and, like the other gods, for Cornutus has become a mere symbol.[70] While there are perhaps certain contacts with the role of Jewish Wisdom,[71] the relationship to early christology is purely formal: the Stoic Logos doctrine is only taken up in Christian thought with the second-century apologists. The Logos of the prologue to the Gospel of John is not the abstract, divine 'world-reason', but the creative word of God's revelation. As such it is dependent on the Jewish Wisdom tradition and not on the Stoa (see below, pp. 48ff., 71ff).

I am indebted to A. D. Nock for three further instances.[72] The first is a late text from the Hermetica. Here, at the request of the elements, Osiris and Isis are sent into the world by the supreme God to bring order out of moral chaos. After they have created a civilized order on earth as *prōtoi heuretai*, i.e. as bringers of culture, they are recalled to heaven. According to Nock, this is 'perhaps a counterblast to Christian teaching, and meant to suggest, "Our gods had an incarnation long ago, in a manner not repugnant to philosophic reason." '[73]

The second instance concerns *Pythagoras*. He was identified by his followers with *Apollo Hyperboreios*,[74] and at a very early stage he was also said to be the offspring of Apollo. In addition, the biography of Iamblichus about AD 300 mentions various divine figures whose earthly manifestation he was thought to be. It was his task to bring men the blessings of philosophy. Of course, in his case it is hard to distinguish the idea of the transmigration of souls

[70] *Theol. graec.* 16 (Wendland, 113), cf. E. Schweizer, *Beiträge zur Theologie des Neuen Testaments*, 1970, 83f. = *ZNW* 57, 1966, 199f.; A. D. Nock, *Essays*, 2, 934.

[71] M. Hengel, *Judaism and Hellenism*, I, 162, cf. also pp. 48ff., 51ff. below.

[72] *Essays*, 2, 937f.; *Kore Kosmou*, Fr. 23, 62–69, ed. Nock/Festugière, CH 4, 20ff. For the Osiris-Isis aretalogy see H. D. Betz, *ZTK* 63, 1966, 182ff.

[73] A. D. Nock, *Essays*, 2, 937f.

[74] Aristotle, Fr. 191, pp. 154f. Rose, following Aelian, *Ver. hist.* 4, 17, and Iamblichus, *Vit. Pyth.* 31, 140ff.; Porphyry, *Vit. Pyth.* 2, 228 (18.31f. Nauck); cf. F. Taeger, *Charisma* I, 73f.

from the notion of the incarnation of a god. Alexander of Abonuteichus, the founder of a religion, therefore considered himself to
be the incarnation of the soul of Pythagoras and when two followers
asked whether 'he had the soul of Pythagoras ... or another like
it', made his oracular god Glycon reply in hexameters: 'The soul
of Pythagoras waxes at one time and wanes at another; but that
(i.e. his own), with prophetic gifts, is a part of the divine spirit, and
the (divine) Father sent it to support good men. Then it will return
again to Zeus, smitten by Zeus' thunderbolt.'[75]

The third example comes from politico-religious poetry. In his
second ode, *Horace* asks whom Jupiter will choose to expiate the
past guilt of Caesar's murder. After a request to Apollo, Venus and
Mars, Octavian appears as the incarnation of Hermes/Mercury to
avenge Caesar and return once again to heaven. In this form of
political, poetic flattery, the poet is certainly saying no more than
that he regards Augustus as a ruler sent by the gods,[76] a view

---

[75] Iamblichus, *Vit. Pyth.* 30f.; but cf. chs. 7f.: Apollo did not beget
Pythagoras himself, 'no one will, of course, doubt that the soul of Pythagoras was under the guidance of Apollo, either as a companion or in some
other close relationship to this god, and in this way was sent down to men'.
Against H. Braun, *Gesammelte Studien*, 259, n. 47, this is not a question
of the pre-existence or descent of a god, but of the sending of a human
soul. According to Heracleides Ponticus he was said to be descended from
or closely connected to Hermes (Diog. Laert., 8, 4). For Alexander of
Abonuteichus see Lucian, *Alex.* 40, but see 4: Μυθαγόρᾳ ὅμοιος εἶναι ἠξίου.

[76] *Carmina* 1, 2, 29ff., cf. F. Taeger, *Charisma*, II, 166f., and E.
Fraenkel, *Horaz*, 1963, 287ff. He sees the identification of Mercury and
Augustus as 'an inspiration of the poet's' (294):

> *Cui dabit partis scelus expiandi*
> *Iuppiter? Tandem venias, precamur*
> *Nube candentis umeros amictus*
>   *Augur Apollo*
> . . .
> *Sive mutata iuvenem figura*
> *Ales in terris imitaris almae*
> *Filius Maiae, patiens vocari*
>   *Caesaris ultor:*
> *Serus in caelum redeas diuque*
> *Laetus intersis popula Quirini*
> *Neve te nostris vitiis iniquum*
>   *Ocior aura*
> *Tollat . . .*

which we also find held about other ruler figures – e.g. Alexander – and above all in the luxuriant inscriptions in the Greek-speaking eastern part of the empire.[77]

The development of the *Romulus saga*[78] should probably also be understood against the background of this early ruler ideology. Some scholars look for parallels to New Testament christology above all in Romulus' miraculous ascension. The twins Romulus and Remus were seen as sons of Mars; but whereas Remus was killed by his brother Romulus, the saga told how Romulus, the founder of Rome, was caught up into heaven in a miraculous ascension. According to a more rationalistic interpretation, however, like Caesar he was murdered by senators. The development of the saga transformed the ascension into an apotheosis. Whereas Ennius[79] still produces an anonymous eyewitness, Cicero, Livy and later writers know his name; there are also reports of the identification of Romulus with the god Quirinius. In Livy, the glorified Romulus commands the eyewitness Proculus Julius: ' "Tell the Romans the will of Heaven that my Rome shall be the capital of the world . . . and let them know and teach their descendants that no human strength will be able to stand up against Roman arms." When he had said this, he departed on high.'[80]

---

[77] Plutarch, *De fort. aut virt. Alex.* 6 (329C): 'But he believed that he came as a heaven-sent governor to all and as a mediator for the whole world.' 8 (330D): 'But if the deity who had sent Alexander's soul here had not recalled him so quickly, there would (now) be one law over all men and they would look to one justice as a common source of light. But as it is, the part of the world which has not looked upon Alexander has remained without the sun.'

[79] Ennius, *Ann.* 1, 110ff. (ed. J. Vahlen). According to *Ann.* 1, 65, the divine plan which was seen to underlie the foundation of Rome also included Romulus' immortality.

[79] Ennius, *Ann.* 1, 110ff., V. According to *Ann.* 1, 65, V, the divine plan which was seen to underlie the foundation of Rome also included Romulus' immortality.

[80] Livy, 1, 16; see Cicero, *De re pub.* 2, 10, 2; Ovid, *Met.* 14, 805ff. Cf. also 848ff. on the ascension of Romulus' consort Hersilia, who becomes the goddess Hora. My colleague Herr Cancik points out that the title Augustus is connected with the '*augurium augustum*' (Enn., *Ann.* 502) of the saga of Romulus and Quirinius, see Carl Koch, *Religio*, 1960, 94–113 (= *Das Staatsdenken der Römer*, ed. R. Klein, 1966, 39–64).

There is a certain formal analogy here to the accounts of the appearances of the risen Christ in Matthew and Luke and to his ascension. The theme of sending appears in Plutarch: 'It was the will of the gods . . . that I should dwell among men only a short time, build a city destined to be the greatest on earth for power and fame, and then dwell again in the heavens whence I came.' One could read the sending of a pre-existent deity out of this. However, as in his writing on Alexander, Plutarch is only bringing his Middle-Platonic doctrine of souls into play. For he expressly attacks what he considers to be the primitive notion of a physical ascension and quotes Pindar: 'Every man's body is overwhelmed by death, and only his primordial image remains eternal, for that alone comes from the gods.' He adds: 'It comes thence and returns thither, not with the body, but when it has detached itself completely from the body and has become pure and unfleshed and clean.'[81] According to Iamblichus, the soul of Pythagoras was also sent to earth in similar fashion.

A fundamental distinction must be made between ideas of this kind about sending and the notion of '*hidden epiphany*' which we come across, say, in the legend of Philemon and Baucis or among the citizens of Lystra, who after a healing miracle revere Barnabas and Paul and say, 'The gods have come down to us in the likeness of men.'[82] The age-old theme of the visit of the gods in human form already appears in the *Odyssey* (17, 484ff.), where the young men chide one of the wooers who abuses the right of hospitality towards Odysseus in the form of a beggar.

> You are doomed, if he is some god come down from heaven.
> Yes, and the gods in the guise of strangers from afar
> put on all manner of shapes and visit the cities.

[81] Plutarch, *Romulus* 28, 2, 7–9.

[82] Ovid, *Met.* 8, 611ff.; *Fasti* 5, 495; Acts 14.11. Cf. also Themistius, 7, p. 90 (see Wettstein ad loc.): 'Pure and divine forces tread the earth for man's good. They descend from heaven, not in airy form, as Hesiod claims, but clothed with bodies like ours. They take upon themselves a life below their nature for community with us.' However, we may certainly assume that there is Christian influence on this Platonizing rhetorician of the fourth century AD. With Julian, he is concerned for a renewal of pagan religion. See also the Neo-Platonic *Vitae Sophistarum* of Eunapius, p. 468, with the quotation from the *Odyssey* 17, 485.

Philo refers to this example in order to explain the epiphanies of God, or more correctly the forms of his intermediaries in Genesis (cf. Gen. 18.1ff.), at the same time stressing that 'God is not like man' (Num. 23.19), has no form and therefore could not assume a body (*Somn.* 1, 232ff.). However, these examples do not mention sending, nor does God take upon himself human fate and death. True, the Greek gods are born and have human pleasures (sometimes even with human beings), but they can never die. Their bodily form is only 'show', and their immortality distinguishes them even more fundamentally from transitory 'mortals'. *All this gets us no nearer to the mystery of the origin of christology.* Celsus, the enemy of Christianity, does not idly keep reminding us that 'neither a God nor a son of God (θεοῦ παῖς) has descended from heaven or will descend. And if you are talking about angels, tell us what kind they are, whether they are gods or have a different nature? You presumably mean some other kind – the demons.'[83] As A. D. Nock

[83] Origen, *C. Cels.* 5, 2, cf. 4, 2–23, see A. D. Nock, *Essays*, 2, 933, where there is further evidence. In contrast to the gods, demons were partially 'earthbound' (8,60). The angels of Celsus correspond to the δυνάμεις of Themistius. The 'scandal' of christology is clearly expressed in pagan polemic against the peculiar – because without analogy – 'God' of the Christians. See the pagan opponent in Minucius Felix, *Oct.* 10, 3: '*Unde autem vel quis ille aut ibi deus unicus solitarius destitutus . . .?*'; 10,5: '*At autem Christiani quanta monstra quae portenta confingunt . . . ?*' cf. 12,4, etc. According to a series of oracles reported by Porphyry (contained in Augustine, *City of God*, 19, 23), Apollo gave the following answer to the question of a man about how he could dissuade his wife from Christian faith: 'Let her go as she pleases, persisting in her vain delusions, singing in lamentation for a god who died in delusions, who was condemned by right-thinking judges and killed in hideous fashion by the worst of deaths, a death bound with iron.' It is striking that Porphyry already attempts to play off the 'historical Jesus' in neo-Platonic interpretation against the folly of his supporters with their absurd doctrines. Thus Hecate is said to have replied to the question whether Christ was God with the words: 'The immortal soul goes on its way after it leaves the body; whereas when it is cut off from wisdom it wanders for ever. That soul belongs to a man of outstanding piety; this they worship because truth is a stranger to them.' To the further question, 'Why then was he condemned?', the goddess gave the oracular reply: 'The body indeed is always liable to torments that sap its strength, but the souls of the pious dwell in a heavenly abode. Now that soul of which we speak gave a fatal gift to other souls . . . entanglement in error . . . For all that, he himself

rightly stresses, the incarnation of a divine figure and still more his shameful death on the cross was not a 'point of contact', but a 'scandal' and a 'stumbling block'. Celsus, the opponent of the Christians, therefore taunts them that the worship of Jesus is no different from the cult set up by Hadrian for his boy-friend Antinous, who was drowned in the Nile and whom the Egyptians would not identify with Apollo or Zeus at any price (Origen, *C. Celsum* 3, 36). This cult was scandalous and reprehensible even to pagans, and the Egyptians were only forced into it because they were afraid of the emperor (Justin, *Apol.* 1, 29, 4). At least he was so incomparably beautiful that he could be compared with Ganymede, whom Zeus put among the gods in Olympus (Clem. Al., *Protr.* 49, 2), whereas for educated or noble men of antiquity the crucified Jesus was only an expression of folly, shame and hatefulness. In the judgment of the younger Pliny, to worship him was a *'superstitio prava immodica'* and merited appropriate punishment (10, 96, 8). *The 'Hellenization' of Christianity thus necessarily had to lead to docetism.* The humanity and the death of Jesus were only tolerable as 'show'.

III. *The Son of God in ancient Judaism*

After this entirely unsatisfactory result, we must return to the contemporary Jewish sources in which the traditional Old Testament conceptions of the son or sons of God were further developed in a number of ways. Here, of course, it should be noted that religious thought in the motherland and the diaspora after the exile, and even more after Alexander, was increasingly driven towards an encounter with the Greek spirit. We cannot have too much variety in an account of Jewish religious thought at the end of the first century BC. The unique intellectual endowment of the people

---

was devout, and, like other devout men, passed into heaven. And so you shall not slander him, but pity the insanity of men. From him comes for them a ready peril of headlong disaster' (translation by Henry Bettenson, 1972). One might almost suppose that some modern 'christological' outlines are nearer to this neo-Platonic oracle of Hecate than to the New Testament.

which made them able to assimilate new patterns of thought can
already be seen in antiquity.[84] The sources for early Christian
thinking are to be sought primarily here, and not directly in the
pagan sphere.

III.(a)   *Wise men, charismatics and the royal Messiah*

In addition to the collective designation of Israel as son or sons
which we find down to the rabbinic writings, there is also an individual application of the term in Jewish wisdom to particular *wise*
men and *righteous* men, when in earlier texts it was reserved for the
Davidic king:

> Be like a father to orphans,
> and instead of a husband to their mother,
> then God will call you his son,
> will have mercy on you and save you from the grave (Sir. 4.10).

Significantly, the grandson of the writer of the proverb tones it
down in the Greek translation and writes, 'and you will be like a
son of the Most High' (καὶ ἔσῃ ὡς υἱὸς ὑψίστου). Finally, in
later Talmudic texts the *charismatic wonder-worker* or even *the
mystic who is transported to God* is often designated 'son' by God
or addressed as 'my son'.[85] We find a further development in the

---

[84] M. Hengel, *Judaism and Hellenism*; id., 'Anonymität, Pseudepi-
graphie und "Literarische Fälschung" in der jüdisch-hellenistischen
Literatur', in *Pseudepigrapha*, I, Entretiens sur l'Antiquité Classique
XVIII, 1972, 231–329.

[85] This fact is usually overlooked completely in discussions of the history
of religions. But see D. Flusser, *Jesus*, 1968, 98ff.; G. Vermes, *Jesus the
Jew*, 1973, 206ff., and *JJS* 24, 1973, 53f., who refers above all to Hanina
b. Dosa as 'son of God': 'Day by day a *bat qol* was heard saying: "The
whole universe is sustained on account of my son Hanina; but my son
Hanina is satisfied with one kab of carob from one Sabbath eve to
another" ' (Taan. 24b; cf. Ber. 17b; Hull. 86a). Cf. Taan. 25a: God
appears to Eleazar ben Pedath in a dream: 'Eleazar, my son, is it right
that I should begin the whole creation of the world anew . . . ?' Hag. 15b:
God says: 'My son Meir said . . .' Cf. also the Midrash of Moses' Death,
Jellinek, *Bet ha-Midrasch* (reprinted 1967), 1, middle of 121: 'The Holy
One immediately began to soothe him and said to him: My son Moses
. . .', cf. also 119: 'I am God and you are God' (Exod. 7.1). According to
Ber. 7a the high priest Ishmael b. Elisha had a vision of Yahweh in the

Wisdom of Solomon, which comes from the diaspora in Alexandria. The first chapters a description of the suffering of the ideal righteous man, who is persecuted and even killed by the godless:

> If the righteous man is God's son, he will help him,
> and will deliver him from the hand of his adversaries
> (2.18; cf. 2.13, 16).

There are clear parallels here to the passion narrative in the synoptic gospels. Presumably there is some relationship between the suffering wise man and son of God and the 'servant of God' in Isa. 53. After his death the righteous man is counted among the 'sons of God', i.e. the angels (5.5).[86] In the Hellenistic Jewish romance of *Joseph and Asenath*, Asenath, the daughter of an Egyptian priest, and other non-Jews on a number of occasions call Joseph 'son of God' because of his supernatural beauty and wisdom; however his brother Levi only calls him 'one beloved of God', and according to Batiffol's edition he is 'like a son of God'. This is probably meant to express the thought that he belongs to the sphere of God: one might even talk of his 'angelic' character.[87] *A fragment of text from*

---

heavenly Holy of Holies, who addressed him: 'Ishmael my son, bless me.' According to the legend of the ten martyrs (Jellinek 6, 21), Ishmael is addressed by the Metatron, God's vizir, as 'my son'. Presumably in the original form God himself spoke here, for in III Enoch 1.8 God himself says to the angels: 'My servants, my seraphim, my cherubim and my ophanim: cover your eyes before Ishmael, my son, my friend, my beloved.' The designation 'my Son' by God, or 'son of God', must have played some role in charismatic and mystic circles of Palestinian Judaism. Memar Marqah calls Moses *br byth d'lh*, 'son of the house of God' (IV §1, p. 85, Macdonald), and rabbinic literature knows the *'phamiliā^c* of God as a technical term, i.e. the angels as the *'phamiliā^c šel ma^{ca}lā'*, cf. Hag. 13b; Sanh. 99b, etc., see S. Krauss, *Griechische und Lateinische Lehnwörter im Talmud, Midrasch und Targum*, 2, 1899, 463. The term can signify the heavenly hosts and also the heavenly council of the wise (Sanh. 67b). Cf. the prayer 'May it be thy will, O Lord our God, to make peace in the *phamiliā^c* above and the *phamiliā^c* below . . .' (Ber. 16b/17a).

[86] See L. Ruppert, *Der leidende Gerechte*, 1972, 78f., 84, 91; K. Berger, *ZTK* 71, 1974, 18ff.

[87] Joseph and Asenath 6.2–6; 13.10; 21.3; but see 23.10 (= Batiffol 75, 4f.); see M. Philonenko, *Joseph et Aséneth*, 1968, 85ff., who seeks to explain the title from Jewish-Hellenistic wisdom speculation in Egypt. Calling Joseph the son of God does not do away with Jacob's paternity

Cave 4 at Qumran shows that the tradition of the *king* as a 'son of God' was not completely lost. The text has messianic quotations from the Old Testament. Nathan's oracle in II Sam. 7.14, 'I will be his father and he will be my son', is transferred to the 'shoot of David', i.e. the Davidic Messiah, 'who will appear . . . in Zion at the end of days' (4QFlor I, 11f.). Psalm 2 is also quoted a little later, but unfortunately the fragment breaks off in the first few verses, so that Ps. 2.7 does not appear. It follows from another fragment that the birth of the Messiah will be God's work:[88] '. . . when (God) brings it about that the Messiah is born among them' (1QSa 2, 11f.). The messianic reference of Ps. 2.7 and other similar passages is not completely lost even among the *rabbis*, for all their anti-Christian polemic. The term 'son of God' appears often in another text from Cave 4, in Aramaic, which presumably comes from a Daniel apocryphon with eschatological contents. Although it is sixteen years since it was purchased, it has only been published in a provisional and fragmentary form. J. A. Fitzmyer supplements it and translates it as follows:

> [. . . But your son] shall be great upon the earth [O King! All (men) shall] make [peace], and all shall serve [him. He shall be called the son of] the [G]reat [God], and by his name shall he be named. He shall be hailed (as) the Son of God, and they shall call him the Son of the Most High (*brh dy 'l yt'mr wbr 'lywn yqrwnh*). As comets (flash) to the sight, so shall be their kingdom. (For some)

(7.5; 22.4). The nearest parallel to this terminology seems to me to be T. Abraham 12, where Abel, the son of Adam, functions as judge of souls. He sits in heaven on a crystal throne that blazes like fire, as a 'wonderful man, glittering like the sun, like to a son of God' (Recension A: ὅμοιος υἱῷ θεοῦ). Cf. also the promise to Levi in Test. Levi 4, 2: 'The Most High has now heard your prayer, to separate you from unrighteousness and for you to be a son, helper and servant to him.' See J. Becker, *Untersuchungen zur Entstehungsgeschichte der Testament der zwölf Patriarchen*, AGAJU 8, 1970, 263f. According to Ezekiel the Tragedian's drama, God addresses Moses from the burning bush: 'Be of good cheer, my son (ὦ παῖ), and hear my words.' Text in B. Snell, *Tragicorum Graecorum Fragmenta*, I, 293, line 100. According to Josephus, *Antt.* 2, 232, the newborn child Moses is a παῖς μορφῇ τε θεῖος.

[88] Cf. E. Lohse, *TDNT* 8, 361f.; G. Vermes, *Jesus the Jew*, 1973, 197ff. W. Grundmann, in *Bibel und Qumran, Festschrift H. Bardtke*, 1968, 86–111.

year[s] they shall rule upon the earth and shall trample everything (under foot); people shall trample upon people, city upon ci[t]y . . . until there arises the people of God, and everyone rests from the sword.

J. T. Milik supplements the passage in a different way and conjectures that the Seleucid usurper Alexander Balas is the son of God, but Fitzmyer sees him as a Jewish ruler. Nor is it possible to rule out a collective interpretation in terms of the Jewish people, like the Son of Man in Dan. 7.13. The parallels to Jesus as the messianic son of God in Luke 1.32, 33, 35, to which Fitzmyer draws explicit attention, are also interesting. We shall have to wait for the publication of the whole text before drawing further conclusions, and it is possible that the riddle of the text will never be satisfactorily solved. However, it makes one thing clear, that the title 'Son of God' was not completely alien to Palestinian Judaism.[89]

It may, however, be objected that all this has to do with the designation of distinguished men as 'sons of God' and not with the transference of divine nature to a man, much less with statements about pre-existence and mediation at creation. However, there is at least an indication of a connection between a man and the world of heavenly 'sons of God' in the Wisdom of Solomon and Joseph and Asenath. In the following section I would like to discuss two Jewish texts, one from Palestine and one from the diaspora, in which this barrier is clearly broken.

[89] Billerbeck, III, 19ff. There is also evidence there for polemic against the Christian conception of 'the Son'. In Pesikta R.37 (Friedmann, 163a), Jer. 31.20: 'Ephraim is my beloved son', is transferred to the suffering Messiah b. Joseph. After his exaltation he is appointed judge over the peoples. See p. 71 below. In the Targum on Ps. 89.27 God promises the Davidic king, i.e. the Messiah: 'He will call on me: "Thou art my Father, my God and the power of my redemption!" ' *hū' yiqrē li 'abbā 'att* . . .; cf. the κράζειν of the spirit in Rom. 8.15 and Gal. 4.6. The roots of the address 'abba' in primitive Christianity – which certainly goes back to Jesus – could lie here, see below p. 63, n. 116. In Ex. R. 19.7, R. Nathan (about 160) refers Ps. 89.28, 'And I will make him my firstborn', to the Messiah, Bill., III, 258. For the new 'Son of God' text from Qumran see J. A. Fitzmyer, *NTS* 20, 1973/74, 391ff. Milik's interpretation is appearing in *HTR*.

III.(b)   *Jewish mysticism: Metatron*

In the so-called *Third Hebrew Book of Enoch*, which derives from
Jewish mysticism, following Gen. 5.24 the man *Enoch is caught up
into the highest heaven and is transformed into the fiery form of an
angel*. As '*Metatron*' he is set on a throne alongside God, appointed
above all angels and powers, to function as God's vizir and plenipotentiary. He is possibly given the title 'prince of the world',
indeed he is even called the 'little Yahweh'. The parallel to New
Testament statements about the enthronement of the exalted
Christ has long since been recognized,[90] and this passage is also
clearly dependent on the earlier Son of Man tradition which
appears, e.g., in Ethiopian Enoch 70;71. The only difference is that
in the time of the rabbis, titles like Son of Man and Son of God
could no longer be used because of competition with Christianity.
Instead, Enoch is given by God the mysterious designation '*na'ar*',
young man.[91] This could be substituted for christological titles
like 'Son' or 'Son of Man' which could no longer be used. Such a
view would be supported by the rabbinic warning against confus-
ing this Metatron with God himself, as 'his name is like that of his
Lord'.[92] When the rabbinic mystic and later apostate Elisha ben

[90] 'Prince of the world': III Enoch 30.2; 38.3; cf. also Ex. R. 17.4;
Hag. 12b; Yeb. 16b; Hull. 60a, etc.; 'little Yahweh': 12.5; 48C, 7; 48D,
1, no. 102. G. Sholem, *Jewish Gnosticism, Merkabah Mysticism and Talmudic Tadition*, 1960, 44ff., has questioned whether the 'prince of
the world' was originally identical with Metatron. The designation *'ebed*
(YHWH) also appears at 48D, 1, no. 17, see H. Odeberg, II, 28, 174, and
III Enoch 1.4; 10.3; etc. See J. Jeremias, *TDNT* 5, 1968, 688, n. 256.
According to Num. R. 12.12, as heavenly high priest he offers the souls
of the righteous as an expiation for Israel. III Enoch 15 (B), 1, declares
him to be greater than all *'elōhim*. For influence on christology see H. R.
Balz, *Methodische Probleme der neutestamentlichen Christologie*, WMANT
25, 1967, 87–112; O. Michel, *Der Brief an die Hebräer*, KEK ¹²1966, 105;
K. Berger, *NTS* 17, 1970/71, 415. Jaoel in the Apocalypse of Abraham is
a related mediator figure. The Metatron speculation is in turn taken up
by the Gnostic *Pistis Sophia* and the Book of Jeu, see Odeberg, I, 188ff.
[91] III Enoch 2.2; 3.2; 4.1, 10; cf. Odeberg, II, 7f.; I, 80; for Mandaean
parallels, 68f., and gnostic parallels, 191; the latter are evidently dependent
on earlier Jewish speculation. According to Yéb. 16b he is not only *na'ar*,
youth, but also *zāqēn*, old man (Ps. 37.25).
[92] Sanh. 38b; cf. III Enoch 12.5: 'And he called me the little (lesser)
Yahweh in the presence of his whole *phamiliā'* (see above, n. 85), as it is

Abuya saw Metatron enthroned in glory in a vision, he is said to have cried out, 'Truly, there are two divine powers in heaven!' This recognition is said to have been the reason for his apostasy from Judaism.[93] The interpretation given by Akiba of the thrones in Dan. 7.9 shows that analogous conceptions could also be transferred to the Messiah: one is for God and the other is for David, i.e. the Messiah. R. Jose the Galilean retorted indignantly: 'Akiba, how long will you go on profaning the Shekinah . . . ?'[94]

III.(c)   *The Prayer of Joseph*

Of course, even here it can be said that this tradition is an analogy to the exaltation christology and explains the appointment of a man to a godlike status, granting him absolute power to rule, but does not explain *pre-existence* before all time, mediation at creation, sending and incarnation. Further help is given us here by a text from the Greek-speaking diaspora. In his commentary on John, Origen quotes a fragment from a Jewish apocryphon, the so-called Prayer of Joseph. There *Jacob-Israel*, the tribal ancestor of the people of God, appears as an incarnate 'archangel of the power of the Lord and supreme commander among the sons of God'. As such he was 'created before all the works of creation' – together with the other patriarchs Abraham and Isaac – and received from

---

written: 'For my name is in him' (Exod. 23.21). For the connection of other angels with the tetragrammaton see 29.1 and 30.1 and Odeberg, II, 104f. Here we have an analogy to the transference of the title Kyrios (in the LXX originally the Qere for the tetragrammaton) to the exalted Christ. K. Berger, *ZTK* 71, 1974, 19, n. 36, gives a similar verdict; he also refers to Jaoel in Apoc. Abr. 10.

[93] III Enoch 16.2, cf. Hag. 15a. For this sacrilege of the arch-apostate Elisha (= Acher), Metatron is punished with sixty strokes of fire. Here is an interpretation which is hostile to Metatron and denounces this kind of mystical speculation about the heavens as dangerous. For rabbinic polemics against the 'two powers' see H. F. Weiss, *Untersuchungen zur Kosmologie des hellenistischen und palästinischen Judentums*, TU 97, 1966, 324f.

[94] Sanh. 38b, par. Hag. 14a. The messianic interpretation of the Son of Man by Akiba also follows from this. Cf. also Billerbeck, I, 486; above all, the interpretation of Anani in I Chron. 3.24 as 'son of the clouds', i.e. as Messiah. See also the exaltation messianology in Pesikta Rabbati below, p. 71, no. 127.

God the name Israel, 'the man who sees God, for I am the first-born of all living beings to whom God gave life'. He descended incognito to earth; the angel Uriel, who stood far below him, burned with envy against him and fought with him at the river Jabbok (Gen. 32.25ff.), but was overcome by Jacob, who referred to his own incomparably higher status. Exodus 4.22, *'Israel is my firstborn son'*, which is applied collectively to the people of Israel, is evidently interpreted here in terms of a supreme, pre-existent spiritual being (πνεῦμα ἀρχικόν) which takes human form in Jacob and becomes the tribal ancestor of the people of Israel. Jacob-Israel can therefore also proclaim to his sons the whole future of the people of God because he has read it on the heavenly tablets of destiny.[95]

III.(d)   *Pre-existent Wisdom*

Mediation at creation, which we have so far missed, meets us continually in the Jewish wisdom tradition from the third century BC onwards. Wisdom already appears as God's *beloved child, born*

---

[95] Origen, *In Joh.* 2.31, §189f. (GCS 10, 88f.), cf. Origen, *In Gen.* 1.14 (3.9), in Eusebius, *PE* 6, 11, 64 (GCS 43, 1, 356). Text also in A.-M. Denis, *Fragmenta Pseudepigraphorum quae supersunt graeca*, 1970, 61f.; id., *Introduction aux pseudépigraphes grecs . . .*, 1970, 125ff., and the more detailed article by Jonathan Z. Smith, 'The Prayer of Joseph', in *Religions in Antiquity. Essays in Memory of E. R. Goodenough*, 1968, 253–94. Smith stresses the connections with Jewish mysticism and wisdom speculation and points to the Jewish origin of the fragment: 'Rather than the Jews imitating Christological titles, it would appear that the Christians borrowed already existing Jewish terminology' (272). Some rabbis also interpret Exod. 4.22 not primarily in terms of the collective Israel, but in terms of the patriarchs, so e.g. R. Nathan in Ex. R. 19. 7: God says to Moses: 'Just as I have made Jacob a firstborn, for it says "Israel is my firstborn son", so I will make the king Messiah a firstborn, as it says: "I will make him my firstborn" ' (Ps. 89.28). Cf. III Enoch 44.10 (Odeberg): 'Abraham my beloved, Isaac my chosen, Jacob my firstborn.' J. Z. Smith reaches the conclusion: 'The PJ may be termed a myth of the mystery of Israel. As such it is a narrative of the descent of the chief angel Israel and his incarnation within the body and of his recollection and ascent to his former heavenly state' (287). H. Windisch, *Neutestamentliche Studien für G. Heinrici*, UNT 6, 1914, 225, n. 1, already saw the significance of this fragment: its 'phrases recall wisdom speculation in the same way as does Col. 1.15'. Cf. also A. D. Nock, *Essays*, 2, 931f.

before all the works of creation and present at the creation of the world, in the fundamental wisdom hymn of Prov. 8.22ff.:

> When he marked out the foundations of the earth,
> then I was beside him as his darling;
> and I was daily his delight,
> rejoicing before him always,
> rejoicing in his inhabited world
> and delighting in the sons of men (8.29f.).

This unique mediator in creation and revelation acquires a function in Judaism in the Hellenistic period which (with a pinch of salt) might be compared with the Platonic world-soul or the Stoic Logos.[96] It gives the world its order and men their rationality: God himself 'poured her out on all his works' (Sir. 1.9). But the Ben Sira who stressed the universality of Wisdom in this statement also proclaimed its extreme exclusiveness in a way which is only understandable against the background of the spiritual struggle of his time. Wisdom went through earth and heaven but found no dwelling place:

> Then the Creator of all things gave me a commandment,
> and the one who created me assigned a place for my tent.
> And he said, 'Make your dwelling in Jacob,
> and in Israel receive your inheritance.'
> From primal times, from the beginning, I was created (Syr and V),
> and for eternity I shall not cease to exist.
> In the holy tabernacle I ministered before him,
> and so I was established in Zion.
> In the city which he loved like me I found my rest (Syr and V),
> and in Jerusalem (arose) my dominion.
> So I took place in an honoured people,
> in the portion of the Lord, in his inheritance (Syr) (24.8–12).

That is, the supreme mediator figure leaves the heavenly sanctuary and settles in *one* point on earth, the temple on Mount Zion in Jerusalem, the place which the God of Israel has chosen and on which according to prophetic promise the throne of the Messiah is also to stand.[97] However, this exclusive restriction goes still further.

[96] M. Hengel, *Judaism and Hellenism*, I, 153ff., 162ff.
[97] Ibid., 157ff.; J. Marböck, *Weisheit im Wandel*, BBB 37, 1971, 17ff.,

For Ben Sira the divine wisdom is identical with the law of Moses.

> All this is the book of the covenant of the Most High (God),
> the law which Moses commanded us
> as an inheritance for the congregations of Jacob (24.23).

This means that the divine wisdom, a cosmic entity, is sent by God himself to a particular place on earth and at the same time takes the form of the law entrusted to Israel on Sinai. The Jews also took this identification of wisdom and Torah further, at the same time continually stressing its universal, cosmic aspect. For Philo, the Jewish philosopher of religion, as for the rabbis, Wisdom-Torah is comparable to the architectural plan or instrument with which God created the world. Both can also be called '*daughter of God*'.[98] According to Philo, *Quaest. Gen.* 4.97, it is 'daughter of God and first-born mother of the universe'. Whether this designation is merely metaphorical and pictorial or whether the conception of a personified hypostasis can be glimpsed through it is of secondary importance. The two were fundamentally interchangeable. Wisdom is also given comprehensive cosmic significance in the *Alexandrian Wisdom of Solomon*. It is 'a breath of the power of God', 'a pure emanation of the glory of the Almighty', 'a reflection of (his) eternal light', 'an image of his (perfect)

34ff., 63ff.; cf. H. Gese, 'Natus ex virgine', in *Probleme biblischer Theologie, Festschrift G. von Rad,* 1971, 87 = *V om Sinai zum Zion,* 1974, 144f.: 'Wisdom, which became a hypostasis in later wisdom theology, and had to be represented as a child of God created in primal times (Prov. 8.22f.), has a comparable function to the king on Zion as a representative of Yahweh's order. Its identity with Yahweh's revelation to Israel leads to the conception that as the pre-existent divine Logos (Sir. 24.3ff.), like the ark, it can only find a permanent abode on Zion (vv. 7ff.). Thus wisdom theology is at root connected with the messianism associated with Zion, and this connection is presupposed in the relatively early passages in the New Testament which speak of the υἱὸς θεοῦ and the sending of the Son . . . The interpretation of Zion theology in terms of wisdom leads to the idea of the pre-existence of the υἱὸς θεοῦ, and the tradition which saw the time of David as being the primal time and hence, like Micah 5.1, taught the protological origin of the eschatological Messiah, inevitably appeared in a different light.'

[98] M. Hengel, *Judaism and Hellenism,* I, 169ff. For the Torah as 'daughter of God' see ibid., II, 111, n. 418. For wisdom as 'daughter of God' in Philo see *De fuga* 50ff.; *De virtute* 62; *Quaest. Gen.* 4, 97.

goodness'. Here we come up against images and concepts which reappear in the same words in christological statements.[99] On the other hand, Wisdom is not described as a daughter of God, but in even more mythological fashion as his 'cohabitant' (8.3) and 'companion to his throne' (9.4). On the other hand, the righteous man inspired by Wisdom is a 'son of God' (2.18), and Israel too is a 'son of God' (18.13), while the Israelites brought up by Wisdom are 'God's children' (9.4, 7; 12.19, 21; 16.21, etc.). Wisdom is sent out (9.10) in the form of the divine spirit (7.7, 22f.; 9.17f.) and 'enters into holy souls', fills 'friends of God and prophets', i.e. is at work in the holy history of Israel, the children of God (7.27). At the same time, like the Stoic Logos, Wisdom permeates the whole universe (8.1).[100]

III.(e)   *Philo of Alexandria*

Wisdom bears very similar traits in the work of Philo of Alexandria, the Jewish philosopher of religion, who is about a generation earlier than Paul. It should, of course be noted that we cannot presuppose any strictly systematic conceptuality in Philo's work. We must reckon with very free and bold associations. For example, Philo can describe God, the 'demiurge' who created the universe, as 'Father', and the divine reason (ἐπιστήμη), which is identical with Wisdom, as the mother of the world, referring explicitly to the wisdom hymn in Prov. 8.22ff., from which we began. 'Having received the divine seed, when her travail was consummated, she bore the only son who is apprehended by the senses, the world which we see.'[8];[1] Here *Jewish wisdom speculation is connected with*

---

[99] Wisdom 7.25; on this cf. B. L. Mack, *Logos und Sophia*, SUNT 10, 1973, 67–72. However, his one-sided interpretation in terms of Egypt misses the point. We have here the typical terminology of religious Hellenistic *koine*, cf. J. M. Reese, *Hellenistic Influence on the Book of Wisdom and its Consequences*, AnalBibl 41, 1970, 41ff. The author is influenced by popular philosophy and the *Hellenistic* Isis aretalogy, which is substantially different from its earlier Egyptian predecessors. Cf. Heb. 1.3; Col. 1.15; II Cor. 4.6.

[100] Cf. P. C. Larcher, *Études sur le livre de la Sagesse* (ÉtBibl), 1969, 329–414: 'La Sagesse et l'Esprit'.

[101] *De ebr.* 30f.; cf. *De fug.* 109: God as father, and Wisdom, 'through

the Platonic doctrine of creation to be found in the Timaeus. To God
as Father of the universe there corresponds *the world as son.* Here,
however, Philo distinguishes between the *spiritual world of ideas*
and the visible world. The former is the *'eldest and first-born son'*
and as such is identical with the *Logos,* the divine reason in the
world. As mediator between the eternal Godhead and the created,
visible world he is at the same time God's 'image' (εἰκών).[102] Philo
can describe him in many different ways: impersonally as the
'spiritual world' or in personified form as the heavenly high priest,
the sinless mediator, the spiritual primal man, the spokesman, the
archangel, indeed as the second god (δεύτερος θεός), who, neither
created nor uncreated, is God's messenger and ambassador, and
rules the elements and the stars as his governor.[103] The visible
world, on the other hand, is the 'younger son', and time the

whom the universe came into existence', as mother of the High Priest, i.e.
the Logos; similarly *Quod det. pot.* 54. See B. L. Mack, op. cit., 145. For
the whole question see also H. Hegermann, *Die Vorstellung vom Schöpfungsmittler* . . . TU 82, 1961, and H. F. Weiss, *Untersuchungen zur Kosmologie des hellenistischen und palästinischen Judentums,* TU 97, 1966,
248–82. A. S. Carman, 'Philo's Doctrine of the Divine Father and the Virgin
Mother', *AJT* 9, 1905, 491–518, and A. Maddalena, *Filone Alessandrino,*
1970, 298–317: 'Il figlio e il padre'; 345–58: 'Dal figlio al padre'.

[102] In *Conf. ling.* 62f. the *'semah'* = *anatole* of Zech. 6.12, which is in
itself messianic, is interpreted in terms of the eldest and 'first-born son',
i.e. the Logos. For his position as mediator see *Quis rer. div.* 205f. Cf. also
Conf. ling. 146; *De agric.* 51; *De somn.* 1, 215; *Quod det. pot.* 82; *Spec. leg.*
1, 96, etc. For the Logos as *eikon* see F.-W. Eltester, *Eikon im Neuen
Testament,* BZNW 23, 1958, 35ff.

[103] E. Schweizer, *TDNT* 8, 355f.; B. L. Mack, op. cit., 167ff. It is improbable that Egyptian Horus mythology underlines the concept of the
Logos as 'son' and 'image', as Mack supposes. Mack underestimates the
Middle-Platonic tradition in which Philo is situated. The light terminology is too widespread in antiquity for far-reaching historical conclusions to be drawn from it. All attempts to interpret Philo predominantly
in terms of a single cause (Egyptian mythology, theology of the mysteries,
gnosticism, Old Testament and Judaism) are misleading and do not do
justice to the complex synthetic character of Philo's thought. For the
Logos as 'second God' see *Quaest. Gen.* II, 62 = Eusebius, *PE* 7, 13, 1:
'Nothing mortal can be made in the likeness of the most High One and
Father of the universe, but (only) in that of the second God, who is his
Logos'; cf. Rom. 8.32 and H.-F. Weiss, op. cit., 261, n. 8. However, see
the remarks about θεός and ὁ θεός in *Somn.* 1, 228ff., see below, 80f.

'grandson of God'. The 'younger son' also functions as mediator;[104] he can 'teach me as a son about the Father and as a work about the master workman'.[105] Philo is *remarkably restrained in transferring the designation 'son of God' to men*. In *Quaest. Gen.* 1, 92 (on Gen. 6.4) his basis for calling the angels 'sons of God' is that they are incorporeal spirits who are not fathered by a man. He adds the observation that Moses also calls 'good and excellent men' sons of God, whereas he calls the wicked only 'bodies'. In *Spec. leg.* 1, 318, on the basis of a combination of Deut. 13.18 and 14.1, he comes to the conclusion 'that men who "do what is pleasing (to nature) and what is good" are sons of God'. Physical descent plays no part here; in principle this does away with any restriction to the nation of Israel. This restraint of Philo's in transferring the term to men is particularly clear in *Conf. ling.* 145ff. First of all, quoting Deut. 14.1 and 32.18, he stresses that all those who have knowledge of the uniqueness of God are called 'sons of the one God'. This is supplemented in traditional Stoic fashion: they 'hold (moral) beauty to be the only good', in order to destroy what is morally bad, that is, pleasure. Philo then adds a qualification: 'But if there is anyone who is as yet unfit to be called a son of God', then he should submit himself 'to the Logos, to God's first-born, who holds the eldership among the angels', the 'archangel' and the 'one with many names', who is at the same time also called 'beginning, name, word of God, man after the image and the one who sees, namely Israel' (. . . κατὰ τὸν πρωτόγονον αὐτοῦ λόγον, τὸν ἀγγέλων πρεσβύτατον. . . · καὶ γὰρ ἀρχὴ καὶ ὄνομα θεοῦ καὶ λόγος καὶ ὁ κατ' εἰκόνα ἄνθρωπος καὶ ὁ ὁρῶν, Ἰσραήλ, προσαγορεύεται).

Referring to Gen. 42.11, 'We are all sons of one man', i.e. Jacob-Israel, he then stresses that those who 'are not fit to be considered sons of God' may be at least sons 'of the most holy Logos', God's 'invisible image'. This is not a matter of physical descent, but of the 'paternity of souls raised to immortality by virtue' (149). Here the saving function of the Logos is particularly clear. Only he, 'the firstborn of God', can make men worthy of being called 'sons of God' through spiritual rebirth. The interpretation of

---

[104] *Quod deus imm.* 31f.; *De ebr.* 30ff. (quot. Prov. 8.22).
[105] *Spec. leg.* 1, 41.

'Israel', of the man who sees God, as *'archē'* and 'oldest archangel' at the same time sheds light on the Prayer of Joseph, which has already been mentioned, though Philo's language has a stronger philosophical stamp. Evidently speculations of this kind were not unusual in diaspora Judaism.

It is therefore all the more remarkable that Philo hardly ever applies the term 'son of God' to a particular figure in salvation history. Of course he is fond of speaking of spiritual procreation, without a father, and in this context can at one point call Isaac 'son of God', but this predicate is not applied to the historical patriarch. In an allegorical interpretation of his name it means 'the best of all the good emotions', 'inner laughter of the heart', which God 'gives as a means to soothe and cheer truly peaceful souls' (*Mut. nom.* 130f.). The designation is only applied to Abraham at one point, in connection with the interpretation of Gen. 18.17: 'Shall I hide (what I plan) from *Abraham*, my friend (LXX on the other hand only has 'my servant', παῖς μου)?' The wise man who is thus a friend of God 'has passed beyond the bounds of human happiness; he alone is nobly born, for he has registered God as his father and become *by adoption* his only son' (μόνος γὰρ εὐγενὴς ἅτε θεὸν ἐπιγεγραμμένος πατέρα καὶ γεγονὼς εἰσποιητὸς αὐτῷ μόνος υἱός). In connection with this, the wise man is praised, in good Stoic fashion, as the sole true rich man, free man and king (*Sobr.* 56f.).[106]

[106] Cf. *Quaest. Gen.* 4, 29 on 18.33, where the encounter of God with Abraham is depicted as the ecstasy of the wise man. This encounter cannot be of permanent duration, but the wise man must be prepared to return, for 'not everything is to be done by the sons in the sight of the Father . . .' In *Quaest. Gen.* 4, 21, Abraham is called 'my servant', following the LXX of Gen. 18.17, similarly *All. leg.* 3, 18. K. Berger (*ZTK* 71, 1974, 7, and *NTS* 20, 1973/74, 34f., n. 132) would see a Hellenistic-Jewish tradition about an unpolitical kingdom in the interpretation of Abraham as the wise man, the adopted son of God, the rich man, the free man and the king. The (ironic) conclusion of Horace's epistle to Maecenas shows that these themes are based entirely on Stoic tradition (*Ep.* 1, 106ff.):

ad summam: sapiens *uno minor est Iove* dives,
liber, *honoratus, pulcher* rex *denique regum,*
praecipue sanus – nisi cum pitvita molesta est
(unless he is plagued with a cold).

Instead of 'son of God', Philo prefers to use 'man of God' (ἄνθρωπος θεοῦ), which goes back to Old Testament models.[107] This restraint is all the more striking since, probably as the result of Hellenistic influence, the boundaries between the divine world and man are blurred in the case of individual figures like the patriarchs and Moses. Thus in *Quaest. Ex.* 2, 29 he interprets the statement in 24.2 that Moses alone is allowed to approach God as meaning that the soul, inspired by God with prophetic gifts, 'comes near to God in a kind of family relation, for having given up and left behind all mortal kinds, it is changed into the divine, so that such men become kin to God and truly divine.' In *Quaest. Ex.* 2, 46 Philo calls this transformation a 'second birth', incorporeal and without involving a mother, brought about through the 'Father of the universe' alone. [108] In an 'eschatological' tractate *De praem. et poen.* 165ff., finally there is a description of the miraculous return of Israel, in which three 'Paracletes' are involved to achieve 'reconciliation with the Father' (πρὸς τὸν πατέρα τακαλλαγαί): God's goodness, intercession and the reformation of those returning home. They have 'no other goal than to find favour with God, *as* sons may with their father'.

Although Philo accordingly does not use 'son of God' frequently in his great work, the term has a considerable breadth of variation. In the cosmic sphere, where its focal point is to be found, it takes

---

Thus already E. Bréhier, *Les idées philosophiques et religieuses de Philoe d'Alexandrie*, ³1950, 233ff.: 'Le fils de Dieu . . . n'est donc que le sage au sens stoïcien, sans qu'il y ait trace d'une relation personelle.'

[107] The designation 'maɹ of God' can be used simultaneously both for the Logos, i.e. the heavenly primal man, and for the wise man who lives in accord with the Logos. For the term cf. LXX Deut. 33.1; Josh. 14.6 = Moses; I Kingd. 2.27; 9.7–10 = Samuel; III Kingd. 12.24; 13.4–31; 17.24; IV Kingd. 1.9–13, etc. = Elijah; 4.7ff. = Elisha. For Philo, see Bréhier, op. cit., 121ff. In I Enoch 15.1, the Enoch who is transported to God in heaven is ὁ ἄνθρωπος ὁ ἀληθινός (or τῆς ἀληθείας).

[108] For Philo's teminology see R. A. Baer Jr, *Philo's Use of the Categories Male and Female*, ALGHJ 3, 1970, especially 55ff.: 'The divine impregnation of the soul.' The regular description of God and the powers subordinate to him as spiritual begetters is intended to present him as 'the source of all goodness and virtue' (61). Salvation history with its individual specific figures retreats right into the background in the face of this present, mystical relationship with God.

up the speculations of Jewish wisdom and of Plato's *Timaeus*; its application to men is usually prompted by Old Testament statements, though they are interpreted in Stoic fashion. Despite the strong Hellenistic stamp, this restraint in the use of metaphor might be connected with a concern to preserve God's transcendence over the world. Of course it stands in striking contrast to Philo's favourite speculations about a 'begetting' or a 'birth' from God. Statements from the Old Testament and Judaism and Hellenistic mythology or philosophy flow into one another almost without a break: in this way Philo shows the wide possibilities of a Greek interpretation of Jewish tradition.

6

The Problem of the Rise
of Early Christology

We have sketched out extremely briefly Jewish terminology relat-
ing to the Son of God and the thought-patterns involved with it:
pre-existence, mediation at creation and sending into the world. It
would seem that there is substantial building material here which
would be used by the early church in the conception of its christological outlines. The remarkable number of names applied to
Wisdom and the various ways of conceiving of it, and even more
the similar variety in the case of Philo's Logos, show us that it is
misleading to unravel the web of christological titles into a number
of independent and indeed conflicting 'christologies', with different
communities standing behind each. To adopt this approach brings
one as near to historical reality as if one were to suppose that there
was an independent 'Logos doctrine' behind each of the names
given to Philo's Logos. Such a method only opens up a wide range
of historical absurdities. This should also be noted in connection
with the rise of christology. Ancient man did not think analytically
or make differentiations within the realm of myth in the way that
we do, but combined and accumulated his ideas in a 'multiplicity of
approximations'. The more titles were applied to the risen Christ,
the more possible it was to celebrate the uniqueness of his saving
work.[109] We should also remember that in the sources which we
possess, as elsewhere in antiquity, we have only a very small, and

[109] Philo says that Logos and Wisdom have 'many names': *Conf. ling.*
146: 'But if anyone is not worthy to be called son of God, let him strive
to take his place under the Logos, his (God's) first-born, the eldest among
the angels, who is archangel and has many names (πολυώνυμος).' According to *Leg. all.* 1, 43, the 'exalted heavenly wisdom' which is identical with
the Logos or described as his mother is said to have many names. Moses

often quite fortuitous, section from a very much larger range of tradition.

The question now is, how far can this mosaic collection of Jewish sources help us to make a hypothetical reconstruction of the development of the Son of God christology in the brief twenty years between the primal event of the death and resurrection of Jesus on which the community was founded and the development of Paul's mission after the apostolic council?

First and foremost, we must remember that what happened cannot just have been a simple reproduction of earlier Jewish speculations about hypostases and mediators. Earliest christology has a quite original stamp, and is ultimately rooted in the contingent event of the activity of Jesus, his death and resurrection appearances. A history-of-religions comparison can only explain the

---

(*Mut. nom.* 125) and the wise man (*Ebr.* 82), and indeed 'divine powers' (*Somn.* 2, 254), have the same epithet applied to them. That in the view of antiquity to have many names was an indication of superior status is evident not only from the way in which seventy names are conferred on Metatron (III Enoch 3.2; 4.1; 48D, 1, 1, 5, 9) but also from the multiplicity of the names of God himself, III Enoch 48B, cf. Philo, *Decal.* 94. The 'pluriform name of God' (τὸ τοῦ θεοῦ πολυώνυμον ὄνομα) should not be wantonly misused. Whereas divine anonymity was seen to be a sign of primitive peoples, multiplicity of names was seen to be a sign of honour: for the Stoa see Diogenes Laert., 7, 135, 147; Ps. Aristot., *De mundo* 7 (401a, 13ff.). Cf. already *Hom. Hymn. Dem.* 18, 32, 'The son of Kronos with the many names' (= Hades), and the appeal to Dionysus 'of the many names' (Sophocles, *Ant.* 1115), Cleanthes, *Hymn to Zeus*, line 1 (SVF 1, 121, lines 34f.): 'Zeus, supreme among the immortals, ruler of the universe, with the many names', and Aristides, *Or.* 49, 29ff. (Keil, 346): 'Zeus has received all the great names which befit him.' 'Isis of the many names' is well-known: Apuleius, *Met.* 11, 5, 2: *cuius numen unicum multiformi specie, ritu vario, nomine multiiugo totus veneratur orbis.* See also the great Isis aretalogy, POx 1380. For the whole matter see E. Bickerman, 'Anonymous Gods', *Journal of the Warburg Institute* 1, 1937/38, 187ff.: H. Bietenhard, *TDNT* 5, 298f. The connection of the many names of Wisdom and the Logos in Philo with the Egyptian Isis aretalogy in B. L. Mack, op. cit., 110, n. 2, is one-sided. This is a very widespread phenomenon. For christology see H. von Campenhausen in connection with the Fourth Gospel, *ZNW* 63, 1972, 220f.: 'This abundance of "names" is no doubt deliberate. Jesus himself in his uniqueness is the sole content of the Gospel. Each possible title is no more than a reference, and none can describe Jesus completely as he is in truth.'

derivation of individual themes, traditions, phrases and functions, and not the phenomenon of the origin of christology as a whole. At the same time, we must also consider the possibility of 'unparalleled' innovation. Even now we have not really progressed very far beyond a judgment which is particularly significant because it was made by such a distinguished scholar of Hellenistic religion as A. Deissmann: 'The origin of the cult of Christ (and that means, of christology) is the secret of the earliest Palestinian community.' Our considerations will have to begin here.

I. *The early confession in Romans 1.3f.*

First of all, I would like to go back to a Pauline text about the Son of God which I have so far kept in the background. The unanimous opinion of scholars is that it contains an early confession. Paul quotes it in the introduction to his letter to the Romans, a community which he did not found. Perhaps he uses this formula to indicate the common creed which they shared. At this point Paul says two things about the 'Son of God' who is the content of his gospel:

> Who was descended from the seed of David according to the flesh and designated Son of God in power according to the Spirit of holiness by his resurrection from the dead (Rom. 1.3f.).

In recent years, more has been written about this than about any other New Testament text.[110] We may spare ourselves the trouble of reporting the many hypotheses about the development of the formula. All attempts at reconstruction are more or less hypothetical. It is clear that two contrasting statements are set side by side here, both of which concern the Son of God (περὶ τοῦ υἱοῦ αὐτοῦ, 1. 3a):

---

[110] See the list in E. Käsemann, *An die Römer*, 1973, 2; K. Wengst, *Christologische Formeln und Lieder des Urchristentums*, SNT 7, 1972, 112ff. G. Eichholz, *Die Theologie des Paulus im Umriss*, 1972, 123ff.; E. Brandenburger, *Frieden im Neuen Testament*, 1973, 19ff. E. Schweizer, *Neotestamentica*, 1963, 180ff.; P. Stuhlmacher, *EvTh* 27, 1967, 374–89, are still important.

1. His human descent is through David. This gives the earthly basis of his messianic status in the context of salvation history.

2. However, the emphasis is on the second expression. By virtue of the resurrection – or chronologically, after the resurrection – he is appointed Son of God in 'divine' power (δύναμις) and in a 'spirit-like', i.e. heavenly, mode of being, which shares in the divine glory.

It would therefore be too one-sided to seek to understand being a Son of God only in 'legal' and 'non-physical' terms.[111] This modern alternative is inadequate. For to talk of Jesus as Son of God is at the same time to make a statement about the 'transcendent' being of the risen Christ with God in his glory, into which he has been 'transformed'. However, in this formula it is striking that Paul does not speak expressly of the pre-existence and sending of the Son, although he may presuppose it in the introduction; indeed from the isolated wording scholars infer that the appointment as Son of God is only brought about through the resurrection from the dead. We may conclude from this that here we really do have a very early confession which is 'pre-Pauline' in the strict sense of the term. It might presumably go back in a simpler form to the first Jewish-Christian community in Jerusalem. H. Schlier suggested as its original form:

> Jesus Christ of the seed of David,
> appointed Son of God
> through the resurrection of the dead.[112]

Paul, on the other hand, certainly understands it in terms of his theology of pre-existence which we find, for example, in the Philippians hymn, where the crucified Christ is given the title 'Kyrios' in the act of exaltation. The nearest Jewish parallel would be the exaltation, transformation and enthronement of the man Enoch, who is also addressed by God with a wealth of titles, including that of 'the little Yahweh'.

---

[111] H. Conzelmann, *An Outline of the Theology of the New Testament*, 1969, 105.

[112] H. Schlier, 'Zu Rö 1, 3f', in *Neues Testament und Geschichte. Festschrift O. Cullmann*, 1972, 207–18, here 213.

II. *The historical background to Romans 1.3f.*

The two-membered confession shows the twofold root of christology extremely well.

The first root is the earthly Jesus from the seed of David. The expression in the first member describes him as Messiah designate. As such he goes to his death. Over his cross, as the political statement of his crime, stood the words 'King of the Jews'. This title runs through the whole passion narrative like a scarlet thread and cannot therefore simply be rejected as a late construction by the community.[113] The early Christian formulations of belief go on to repeat in numerous variations the claim that 'The Messiah (Christ) died for us' or 'for our sins'. The shameful death of the Messiah-designate was an unheard-of scandal which from the beginning compelled the primitive community to interpret this horror in terms of the need for it if the Old Testament promise of salvation were to be fulfilled. This is not, of course, the question here. The death of Jesus is only presupposed implicitly in the statement about the resurrection.

[113] M. Hengel, *Nachfolge und Charisma*, BZNW 34, 1968, 42ff. That the charge of being 'king of the Jews' was tantamount to rebellion in the eyes of the Roman administration is shown by the characterization of the Jewish kings in Tacitus, *Hist.* 5, 8: '*Tum Iudaei Macedonibus invalidis, Parthis nondum adultis (et Romani procul erant), sibi ipsi reges imposuere.*' Only the Romans had the right to appoint and depose kings within their empire, see Josephus, *BJ* 1, 282: Mark Anthony is resolved 'to make Herod king of the Jews'. On the other hand, according to *Antt.* 14, 384, the Hasmonean Antigonus forfeited his kingdom because he had been appointed by the Parthians. According to Dio Cassius 49, 22, 6 he was executed as a rebel by the axe, having been first bound to a stake and flogged, 'which is something that no king of the Romans had suffered' (cf. Strabo, according to Josephus, *Antt.* 15, 9). For the mockery of Jesus as 'king of the Jews' see not only the Carabas episode in Alexandria (Philo, *In Flacc.* 36ff.), but also the order of Lupus, the Prefect in Alexandria, to mock a Jewish king (Andreas Lukuas of the rebellion of AD 116–117?) in a mime in the theatre, see the *Acta Pauli et Antonini*, col. 1, 1, 4f., *Acta Alexandrinorum*, ed. Musurillo, 1961, 37. We cannot overestimate the scandal of a crucified *Jewish* Messiah king who was to be proclaimed 'Lord' and 'Son of God'. Pilate's question (Mark 15.9, 12), and still more the *titulus* on the cross, are expressions of hostility to Judaism. For the interpretation of the title 'king' and Davidic sonship in charismatic terms and in terms of wisdom see K. Berger, *ZTK* 71, 1974, 1–15.

The event of the resurrection makes up the second root of christology and its immediate offence. God acknowledged the condemned man on the cross. So the statement 'God has raised Jesus' could be described as the real primal Christian confession which keeps recurring in the New Testament – even more often than the formula of the dying of Christ.[114] The passive participle ὁρισθείς in Rom. 1.4 is a typical divine passive, which is a periphrasis of God's own action. It should be noted here that the resurrection by itself is inadequate to explain the origin of Jesus' messiahship. The exaltation of a martyr to God was by no means an indication of his eschatological and messianic, i.e. his unique, status. The resurrection is especially significant because here God confirms the crucified 'king of the Jews', his anointed.[115] He brings about this confirmation by appointing Jesus Son of God, by virtue of the resurrection from the dead. And so we come to the question which particularly interests us: why does the confession read 'Son of God' at this decisive point and not 'Son of Man', or 'Messiah', or even 'Lord'? We would really expect another title in the context of the exaltation of Jesus: in Ethiopian Enoch 71.14, God addresses the exalted Enoch: 'You are the Son of Man who is born for righteousness', and Ps. 110, which is quite decisive for early christology, begins: 'The Lord said to my Lord, Sit at my right

---

[114] From the flood of literature on the resurrection, see B. Rigaux, *Dieu l'a ressuscité*, 1973, esp. 311ff.; P. Stuhlmacher, 'Das Bekenntnis zur Auferweckung Jesu von den Toten und die Biblische Theologie', *ZTK* 70, 1973, 365–403, and the third number of *TQ* 153, 1973, on 'the origin of resurrection faith', with contributions by R. Pesch, W. Kasper, K. H. Schelkle, P. Stuhlmacher and M. Hengel.

[115] Cf. N. A. Dahl, 'Der gekreuzigte Messias', in H. Ristow – K. Matthiae, *Der historische Jesus und der kerygmatische Christus*, 1960, 161: '. . . it could be concluded from the appearances of the risen Jesus that he was alive and had ascended into heaven, but not that he was the Messiah . . . The resurrection meant that Jesus had been put in the right by God over against his adversaries. Had he been crucified for messianic claims, then – and only then – belief in his resurrection would have had to become belief in the resurrection of the crucified Messiah.' Similarly J. Jeremias, *New Testament Theology*, I, 255: 'Faith in the resurrection of a murdered messenger of God certainly does not amount to belief in his messiahship (cf. Mark 6.16). Furthermore, the scandal of the crucified Messiah is so enormous that it is hardly conceivable that the community should have presented itself with such a stumbling block.'

hand . . .' The keyword 'Lord' appears here as in Philippians. The Old Testament and Jewish statements about the Son of God are, as we saw, both confusingly varied and very obscure: in contemporary Judaism in particular, 'Son of God' is not really used as a title for the Messiah. A first reply to this might be: more than any other title in the New Testament, the title Son of God connects the figure of Jesus with God. He is the beloved (Mark 1.11; 9.7; 12.6 par.), the only (John 1.14, 18; 3.16, 18; I John 4.9) and the first-born Son (Rom. 8.29; Col. 1.15, 18; Heb. 1.6; cf. Rev. 1.5). This is meant to express the fact that in Jesus, God himself comes to men, and that the risen Christ is fully bound up with God. It may now be objected that this apparently dogmatic information does not add up to a historical proof. There are, however, good historical reasons for it, of which I will name four:

1. An important starting point is Jesus' unique relationship with God, expressed in the address 'Abba', 'dear Father', which it was quite unusual for a Jew to use to God. This alien Aramaic word is a form of address which Paul himself hands on to the communities he founded, and is a sign, effected by the Spirit, that the Son makes believers sons of God. Even if Jesus probably did not designate himself 'Son of God' in so many words, the real root of this post-Easter title lies in his filial relationship to God as Father.[116]

2. A further root is the messianic argument from scripture. Jesus was denounced by the leaders of the people to Pilate as an alleged messianic pretender and condemned to death by Pilate. In the events of the resurrection, the oldest testimony to which is Paul's formal account in I Cor. 15.3ff., the early community saw

---

[116] Rom. 8.15; Gal. 4.5f.; Mark 14.36. J. Jeremias, *The Prayers of Jesus*, SBT II 6, 1967, 11–65; id., *New Testament Theology*, I, 1971, 61ff., 178ff. The original form of the revelation saying in Matt. 11.27 = Luke 10.22 is also an expression of this filial relationship, see op. cit., 56ff. The attempt by K. Berger, *NTS* 17, 1971, 422ff., to derive it from the wisdom tradition of teaching and the understanding of 'teacher' and 'pupil' is, on the other hand, too one-sided. Like Gal. 4.4ff., Rom. 8.15ff. shows that the theme here is the eschatological liberation of the children of God. This already has its roots in Jesus' preaching of the 'kingdom of God' and in his actions. The only explanation of the significance of the Aramaic cry 'Abba' in Paul's Gentile-Christian communities is that it goes back to Jesus himself. See also p. 45, n. 89 above, on Ps. 89.27.

the divine confirmation of Jesus' messianic claim. However, this Messiahship of the crucified, risen and exalted Jesus went completely counter to the popular, traditional expectation of a political liberator and learned exponent of the Torah, which is the expectation that had been put about especially by Pharisaism. The missionary preaching of the first witnesses of the resurrection to their own people derived the force of its argument in the first place from 'scriptural proof', which put prophetic promise before the Torah. Thus it was possible to read the conjunction of resurrection and the divine sonship of Jesus out of the ancient oracle given by Nathan to David (II Sam. 7.12–14): 'I will raise up your seed after you (*wah^aqimōtī* = καὶ ἀναστήσω) . . ., and I will establish his kingdom. He shall build a house for my name, and I will establish the throne of his kingdom for ever. I will be his father, and he shall be my son.' My friend Otto Betz has clearly shown that the interpretation of II Sam. 7.12ff. in terms of the risen Christ clearly lies behind the early confession in Rom. 1.3f.[117] There are further indications of the strong influence of II Sam. 7.12–16 on the developing christology of the primitive community in Luke 1.32f.; Acts 13.33f.; Heb. 1.5, for there is the history of an earlier tradition behind all these passages. In addition, II Sam. 7.14 is very closely associated with Ps. 2.7 in the last two passages. A connection between Messiah and Son of God also followed clearly from Ps. 2 and Ps. 89. Moreover, as 'Son of God' could be used both for the suffering righteous man and for the charismatic and the wise man, why should this designation not have been transferred quite deliberately to the exalted Messiah Jesus? Thus a variety of lines of tradition come together in the title 'Son of God'.

3. Jesus spoke in a mysterious way of the coming 'Son of Man' (Aramaic *bar ^enās*), and 'identified' himself with this figure of the judge to come: I also believe that in the end he was able to speak

[117] O. Betz, *What do we know about Jesus?*, 1968, 87ff., 96ff. Cf. also E. Schweizer, 'The Concept of the Davidic "Son of God" in Acts and its Old Testament Background', in L. E. Keck/J. L. Martyn (eds.), *Studies in Luke-Acts*, 1966, 186–93. For a fundamental discussion of the messianic proof from scripture in relation to the death and resurrection of Jesus see also J. Jeremias, *Abba*, 1966, 205, on the influence of Isa. 53 (which is hardly to be doubted).

of himself in veiled form as 'the (Son of) Man'. This is the only explanation of how this mysterious title was given such a central significance in all the gospels as an exclusive self-designation of Jesus, although it was not a current messianic title, and for that reason evidently could not be used in early Christian mission preaching either. It has no real kerygmatic significance. True, there is mention in the synoptic gospels of the suffering Son of Man and the Son of Man who is to come, but not of belief in him. The two contemporary Jewish texts which speak of the Son of Man already identify him with the Messiah.[118] Things were no different in primitive Christianity. The resurrection served only to a limited degree as proof for the truth of Jesus' proclamation of the Son of Man: God has shown that the crucified Jesus is himself the Son of Man, and as such he will return in the function of judge and bringer of salvation. Now on linguistic grounds alone it would seem obvious, by the law of analogy, that the bar *'eenās(ā)* (Son of Man) who had been confirmed and exalted by God should also be confessed as bar *'elāh(ā)* (Son of God). This was all the more likely since the 'Son of Man' had at the same time been exalted over all the heavenly 'sons of God' and had all power given into his hand as God's eschatological 'plenipotentiary'. The development which has been outlined here with the utmost brevity, leading to the statement contained in Rom. 1.3f. about the Son of God who is appointed through the resurrection, may have taken place in Palestine itself in a relatively short time. Its foundation lay in the inner consistency of a combined consideration of the preaching and actions of Jesus, his death and the event of the resurrection. Paul, in describing his call near Damascus, which took place between AD 32 and AD 34, as a revelation of the Son of God by God himself, is in my view already presupposing the central significance of this title for that time.[119] In the vision he sees at his call, he is sure of 'the

---

[118] Eth. Enoch 48.10; 52.4; IV Ezra 13; cf. U. B. Müller, *Messias und Menschensohn in jüdischen Apokaeypsen und in der Offenbarung des Johannes*, SNT 6, 1972, 52ff., 81ff., 111ff. For the rabbinical exegesis of Dan. 7.13 see Billerbeck, I, 486, and Justin, *Dial c. Tryph.* 32.

[119] Gal. 1.15f.; see n. 19 above. Cf. M. Hengel, in *Neues Testament und Geschichte, Festschrift O. Cullmann*, 1972, 62.

identity of the heavenly Messiah with the crucified Jesus'.[120] Jesus, the son of David, was none other than the risen Son of God. The message of the Christians against which Paul the Pharisee and the scribe fought so bitterly was not a diabolical deception, but God's eschatological truth.

4. This development towards the use of υἱὸς θεοῦ as a central honorific title was strengthened by the fact that it was possible to translate the Hebrew ʿ*ebed* with παῖς and then interpret it as 'Son'. This explains why 'servant of God' (παῖς θεοῦ) as a christological title has already faded right into the background in the New Testament texts. But we may assume that its influence in earliest Christianity was never as strong as is sometimes supposed. It is, for instance, questionable in the extreme whether υἱὸς θεοῦ in the baptism pericope in Mark 1.11 has suppressed an original παῖς θεοῦ.[121] Thus the confession 'Son of God' is primarily an explicit expression of Jesus' *exaltation*.

III. *Pre-existence, mediation at creation and sending into the world*

But how are we to explain the move towards ideas of *pre-existence, mediation at creation* and the *sending* of the Son of God into the world, which already have central significance for Paul?

[120] J. Weiss, *Earliest Christianity*, I, 1937 reprinted 1959, 191 (italicized by the author), cf. 161. We do not know whether Paul, as a Pharisee of the Diaspora, already believed in the existence of a heavenly messianic figure and if so, in what form. Conjectures were made by the history of religions school (they were particularly crass in e.g. M. Brückner, *Die Entstehung der paulinischen Christologie*, 1903) about a pre-Christian Hellenistic Jewish speculation concerning a pre-existent heavenly *Messiah*, but they have no direct foundation in any sources known to us. We only have access to the wisdom tradition. Of course, the literature of Hellenistic Judaism is almost completely lost, apart from Philo, Josephus and a few small fragments. We do not know, for example, what traditions lie behind the revelation of the eschatological high priest (T. Levi 18). On the other hand, the assumption of a pre-Christian Jewish 'Christ-gnosis', as suggested by W. Schmithals, is quite without foundation.

[121] Cf. J. Jeremias, *Abba*, 1966, 191–216. For the pericope about Jesus' baptism (Mark 1.9–11) see F. Hahn, *Christologische Hoheitstitel*, 1963, 301ff., 340ff.; this is questioned by F. Lentzen-Deis, *Die Taufe Jesu nach den Synoptikern*, 1970, 186ff., 262ff.

It is possible and indeed probable that they were first developed among those Greek-speaking Jewish Christians who were driven out of Jerusalem and began the mission to the Gentiles in the Hellenistic cities of Palestine, Phoenicia and Syria. On the other hand, Paul already uses these expressions as though they had established forms. Direct pagan influence is extremely improbable, if only because of the ethnic composition of these earliest mission communities. The Jewish Christians were always the spiritual driving force which determined the content of the theology. In fact they put their stamp on the whole of the first-century church. Unfortunately the history of religions school paid too little attention to this decisive point. The men who carried on the spiritual controversy with Judaism most sharply during the first century AD come from Judaism: Stephen; the Pharisee Paul; and the authors of the First, Second and Fourth Gospels, Hebrews and Revelation. Another predominant group was that of the so-called God-fearers, who were already closely associated with Judaism before their change to the new faith: the author of the Third Gospel and Acts may well come from their circles.[122]

There is also an *inner consistency* in the further development of christology. The confession of the exaltation of Jesus as Son of Man and Son of God in the resurrection and his appointment as God's eschatological plenipotentiary immediately posed for earliest Christianity the question of the relationship of Jesus to other intermediary figures, whether the supreme angels or Wisdom-Torah, which was at least partially thought of as a personification. It was also necessary to reconsider the relationship between the previous means of salvation in Judaism, temple worship and the Torah, and the exalted Son of God and mediator of salvation. This led to a critical distinction between Christianity and Judaism.[123] Certainty

[122] F. Siegert, 'Gottesfürchtige und Sympathisanten', *JSJ* 4, 1, 1973, 109–64; M. Hengel, 'Zwischen Jesus und Paulus', *ZTK* 72, 1975, 151–206.

[123] Against Klaus Berger, *Die Gesetzesauslegung Jesu*, WMANT 40, 1972, 17ff., we do not find within the pre-Christian Judaism of the diaspora, let alone in Palestine, a real and fundamental criticism of the law, that is, one with a religious motivation, which, say, rejected the whole of the ritual law and concentrated only on the moral commandments. The

that the 'time of the Messiah' had dawned in the works, death and
resurrection of Jesus also provided the impulse for a fundamental
change of attitude towards the law of Moses. The true will of God
was no longer embodied in the Torah of Sinai but in the teaching
of the Messiah Jesus, and his accursed death on the cross (Deut.
21.23) could and indeed must put in question the law of Moses as
an *ultimate* authority. Even in a messianic context, the exodus and
the revelation of the law on Sinai was the real, normative saving
event. Christians now consistently transferred it to the person of
Christ and his work. The statement at the end of the Torah (Deut.

---

radical reformers in Jerusalem after 175 BC strove for complete assimilation
to paganism, and this was also usually the aim of a Jew who broke with
the law of the fathers. The Jewish critics of the law of whom Philo speaks
(*Agr.* 157; *Vit. Mos.* 1, 31; *Conf. ling.* 2ff.), or the radical allegorists (*Migr.
Abr.* 89ff.), were on the fringe of Judaism and hardly had any influence
worth mentioning, see H. A. Wolfson, *Philo*, 1, ³1962, 82ff., and I. Heine-
mann, *Philons griechische und jüdische Bildung*, 1932 reprinted 1962, 454ff.
At the decisive initial stage, the early Christian criticism of the law was
hardly influenced by this lax assimilative Judaism. Paul does not idly call
himself a former 'Zealot' for the tradition of the fathers (Gal. 1.14). On
the other hand, the early Christian criticism of the law which emerges in
Palestine itself is not oriented on secular emancipation but entirely on a
new radical understanding of the will of God. In other words, it must have
had an eschatological basis, and ultimately goes back to an original authority, namely Jesus himself. Of course, a reference to a 'new Torah of
messianic times' is also questionable (against W. D. Davies, *Torah in the
Messianic Age and/or the Age to Come*, JBL Monograph Series 7, 1952,
and H. J. Schoeps, *Paul*, 1961, 171ff.). At best the rabbis knew of reflec-
tions on a partial transformation of the law when sin had come to an end,
in connection with the question of the 'grounds of the Torah', see now
P. Schäfer, *ZNW* 65, 1974, 27–42. Paul merely thought through consistently and radically, to the end, the partial criticism of the Torah in a
christological and soteriological perspective which had already been introduced by Jesus and was taken further by the Hellenists of Stephen's
group (Acts 6.11, 13f.). If God's saving revelation in his Christ was really
universal and final, it must also be valid for all men; if God's Christ was
the ground of salvation, then the law of Moses could no longer be regarded as a way to salvation. God's Christ stood above the law which
according to Deut. 21.23 had delivered him over to God's curse. Similarly,
Jesus' sacrificial death made all temple sacrifice meaningless. He alone
was now the propitiatory sacrifice, the sacrifice of the covenant, the atoning sacrifice, the true passover lamb, indeed the high priest and the place
of reconciliation in one. Even the Jewish-Christian Ebionites rejected
sacrifice. See M. Hengel, *ZTK* 72, 1975, 190ff.

34.10): 'And there has not arisen a prophet since in Israel like Moses, whom the Lord knew face to face, none like him for all the signs and the wonders which the Lord sent him to do' is corrected by Jesus in terms of John the Baptist in Luke 16.16 and in terms of himself in Matt. 11.27 = Luke 10.22. The earliest christology must already have robbed it of its force.

Following the well-known saying in the Epistle of Barnabas, 'Behold I make the last things as the first things' (6.13), the eschatological awareness of the earliest community was matched by a certain interest in protology. Only the one who has control over the beginning has the whole matter in his grasp. The beginning therefore *had to* be illuminated by the end, and ultimately the *idea of pre-existence* was a favourite means of bringing out the special significance of particular phenomena for salvation. One might perhaps say that it expressed the common Near Eastern view that there was a correspondence between the heavenly original and earthly reality in typical Jewish fashion, by means of a projection back into primal time. The pre-existence of the eschatological redeemer could already be read out of Micah 5.1 or Ps. 110.3: he was begotten by God, older than the dawn of creation (see n. 49 above). We also find further statements about the pre-existence of the Son of Man in Enoch 48.6; 62.7: he is said to have been elected by God before the creation of the world; there is also mention of the pre-existence of his name (48.3; cf. 69.26). To this corresponds the pre-existence of the name of the Messiah in rabbinic sources.[124] As in the case of the relationship between a personified hypostasis and purely metaphorical language, the transition here from mere 'ideal' pre-existence (that is, to some extent only in the thought of God) to 'real' pre-existence is fluid. Moreover, the concept of 'pre-existence' is not yet understood in the sense it later acquires during the Arian dispute as uncreatedness and timeless, eternal being with God. In the first place it denotes a 'being before the creation of the

[124] Cf. U. B. Müller, *Messias und Menschensohn*, 47ff.: 'Like the Messiah in IV Ezra, the Son of Man in I Enoch is a pre-existent factor in salvation, a part of the world already created by God, which will only appear at the end of time' (49). For the rabbis see Billerbeck, II, 334–52, above all, 335: Pes. 54a Bar.; Targ. Zech. 4.7, etc.; 346f.: speculations about the pre-existent soul of the Messiah from Amoraean times.

world'. Nevertheless, there were also changes here. Thus as early
as Prov. 8.22f., 'being born' also stands alongside verbs about being
created. At least Wisdom or the Logos must always have been
associated with God. Indeed one could not conceive of God without his Wisdom.[125] The more christological reflection progressed,
the more it was inevitably involved in trinitarian questions. According to later rabbinic tradition, reference was made to Gen. 1.2 'and
the spirit of God hovered' to prove the 'pre-existence' of the
Messiah before creation, because this phrase meant the spirit of
the Messiah (Pes. R. 33, 6; cf. Gen. R. 2, 4).[126] A related text

[125] Prov. 8.22: *qānāni* = he created me; 8.23: read *nesakkōti* = 'I was
skilfully made', see H. Gese, in *Probleme biblischer Theologie. Festschrift
G. von Rad*, 1971, 81f. = *Vom Sinai zum Zion*, 138f., who also reads this
form (instead of *nāsakti*, which has the same consonants) in Ps. 2.6: 'But
I was created (in a wonderful way) as his king on Zion . . .'; 8.24: *ḥōlalti*,
'I was born in travail'. Concepts like 'begetting', 'bringing forth', 'reflecting' and 'flowing' are even more predominant in Philo and Wisdom as
over against those of creating and forming. Philo can call the Logos
eternal: 'The head of all things is the eternal Logos of the eternal God'
(*Quaest. Ex.* 2, 117; of course here we could have a Christian interpretation
in the Armenian text, see the continuation. Cf. the *re'šit* in Gen. 1.1;
Prov. 8.22; Col. 1.18; Eph. 1.22; cf. H. F. Weiss, *Kosmologie*, 265ff.).
According to *Quis rer. div. her.* 205f., the 'oldest Logos' and 'archangel',
who was given the task by the Father and Creator of the world 'to divide
the creation from the Creator', was, as mediator, 'neither uncreated like
God . . . nor created (like the creatures), but in the middle between the
two extremes'. As such he is 'spokesman for . . . mortals' and 'the ruler's
envoy to the servants'. 'For like a herald I bring to creatures the message
of peace of the one who has resolved to abolish wars, the God who constantly watches over peace.' The later distinction between the *logos
endiathetikos* and the *logos prophorikos* in Theophilus of Antioch (*Ad
Autolyc.* 2, 10) indeed already goes back to Philo, who developed Stoic
conceptuality in speculative fashion.

[126] According to Gen. R. 2, 4, R. Simeon b. Lakish (middle of the third
century AD) interpreted Gen. 1.2 in terms of the four world kingdoms:
tōhū = Babylon; *bōhū* = the Medes, the kingdom of Haman; darkness =
Javan (Macedonia); the deep (*teḥōm*) = the power of wickedness (Rome).
' "And the spirit of God hovered", this is a reference to the spirit of the
king Messiah, as is said in Isa. 11.2: "The spirit of Yahweh rests upon
him" '; cf. Lev. R. 14.1: 'the spirit of the king Messiah'. On the other
hand, according to Yalqut Ps. 139, §5 (265a), Gen. R. 8, 1 and Midr.
Tanchuma Tarzia (Buber, 153a), Simeon b. Lakish interpreted the spirit
in Gen. 1.2 in terms of the soul of Adam. According to Theodor's edition,
manuscript D likewise has 'king Messiah' in Gen. R. 8, 1 (p. 56). Probably

identifies the primal light of creation in Gen. 1.4 with the light of
the Messiah which God conceals under his throne. At Satan's
request, God shows him the Messiah hidden under the throne,
whereupon Satan falls to the ground, for he has seen his own
annihilation and that of his followers (Pes. R. 36, 1).[127] *Thus there
was an inner necessity about the introduction of the idea of pre-existence
into christology.* Eberhard Jüngel is quite right when, from the
standpoint of a systematic theologian, he passes the judgment: 'It
was more a matter of consistency than of mythology.'[128] With pre-
existence, however, statements about the sending of the Son took
on their fullest form. Angels or men of God and prophets of the
Old Testament had already been said to have been sent by God,
and according to Mal. 3.23 the sending of Elijah is promised for
the end-time; in a similar way the Jewish Sibyl could talk of the
sending of the messianic king.[129] Luke takes up this theme in Acts
3.20: '. . . that times of refreshing may come from the presence of
the Lord, and that he may *send* the Christ appointed for you,
Jesus . . .' Given pre-existence, however, sending now presupposes

---

Simeon b. Lakish put forward both interpretations, and it is illegitimate
simply to push the reference to the Messiah or his soul to one side as an
allegory (as happens in Billerbeck, II, 350). Pes. R. 33, 6 (Friedmann,
152b) shows that the idea continued to exercise influence: 'What is the
proof that the Messiah has existed since the beginning of the creation of
the world? "And the spirit of God hovered." That is the king Messiah! For
we read, "And the Spirit of the Lord will rest on him" (Isa. 11.2).'

[127] Pes. R. 36, 1 (Friedmann, 161a/b). Sections 36 and 37 show the
Messiah ben Ephraim as a pre-existent figure who obediently takes upon
himself the suffering intended by God for the sins of Israel and allows
himself to be sent into the world. After his liberation from suffering he is
exalted, enthroned and glorified by God in heaven. Billerbeck's conjecture
that this homilectic Midrash only came into being about AD 900 is questionable. J. Bamberger, *HUCA* 15, 1940, 425ff., conjectures on the basis
of certain political information that sections 34–37 were composed between 632 and 637. The traditions which it contains are for the most part
considerably earlier. Obviously Christian influence is possible and indeed
probable here. We can, however, see those forms which Jewish messianology was able to accept even after the separation from Christianity and
despite the polemical controversy with it. Would things have been so very
different in the pre-Christian period?

[128] E. Jüngel, *Paulus und Jesus*, ²1964, 283.

[129] Sib. 3, 286 (Cyrus?); 5, 108, 256, 414f.

a descent from the heavenly sphere, humiliation and incarnation as depicted in the Philippians hymn (the analogy is with Wisdom in Sir. 24). It is typically Jewish that in the exposition of christology, pre-existence, mediation at creation and the idea of sending the Son into the world were all developed chronologically *before the legends of the miraculous birth of Jesus*. The tradition behind the prologue to the Fourth Gospel is 'earlier' than the infancy narratives of Matthew and Luke in their present form. That is the most obvious place to talk of 'Hellenistic' influence, even if the form chosen is that of the Jewish Haggadah. Thus the problem of 'pre-existence' necessarily grew out of the combination of Jewish ideas of history, time and creation with the certainty that God had disclosed himself fully in his Messiah Jesus of Nazareth. The 'simple gospel of Jesus' was not, then, delivered over to pagan mythology; on the contrary, the threat of myth was overcome by the radical trinitarian character of the idea of revelation.

Once the idea of pre-existence had been introduced, it was obvious that the exalted Son of God would also attract to himself the functions of Jewish Wisdom as a mediator of creation and salvation. Even Wisdom, which was associated with God in a unique way from before time, could no longer be regarded as an independent entity over against the risen and exalted Jesus and superior to him. Rather, all the functions of Wisdom were transferred to Jesus, for 'in him are hid all the treasures of wisdom and knowledge' (Col. 2. 3). Only in this way was *the unsurpassibility and finality of God's revelation* in Jesus of Nazareth expressed in a last, conclusive way. The exalted Jesus is not only pre-existent, but also shares in the *opus proprium Dei*, creation. Indeed, he accomplishes the work of creation at the behest and with the authority of God, just as he also determines events at the end of time. No revelation, no speech and no action of God can take place without him or beside him. So it is the pre-existent Christ who must accompany Israel on its journey through the wilderness as the 'spiritual rock' (I Cor. 10.4). According to Wisdom 10.17 it was the divine Wisdom which guided Israel on its miraculous journey, and Philo identified the rock from which Moses drew water, like the manna, with Wisdom or the Logos (*Leg. all.* 2, 86; *Det. pot.* 115ff.). Palestinian exegesis, on the other hand, had the people led on their journey through the wilderness by the Shekinah of Yahweh. As the exegesis in I Cor. 10.4 is not typically Pauline, and Paul does not otherwise draw positive connections with the time of Moses – indeed he interprets the consequences of this event to the Corinthians in a negative way – we must assume that this exegesis comes from non-Pauline Greek-speaking Jewish Christianity. The stream of tradition which included this christology influenced by pre-existent Wisdom was surely broader than Paul's letters suggest. The Logos christology of the Johannine prologue about fifty years after Paul is therefore only the logical conclusion of the fusion of the pre-existent Son of God with traditional Wisdom, though of course the concept of '*sophia*', which was always threatened by mythological speculation, had to give place to the clear 'Logos', the Word of God. The prologue, too, is therefore certainly not to be derived from gnostic sources, but stands in an established context of tradition within Christianity and Judaism.[130] The christological climaxes of the Fourth Gospel, like 1.1: '. . . and the Word was with God and the Word was God', or 10.30: 'I and the Father are one', mark the goal and the consummation of New Testament christology.

Now for the Son of God to take on the all-embracing functions of Wisdom as mediator was also to shatter to pieces the function of the law in the ordering of the world and the salvation of men. For the Jews, the law was identified with Wisdom and its functions were authoritative and had an ontological basis. Paul, the former Pharisee and scribe, drew the ultimate radical consequences here. Other people before him had pondered what changes in the law were to be made as a result of the exegesis of the true will of God in the message of Jesus the Messiah, but Paul's pointed expression

---

[130] See already the considered criticism by W. Eltester, 'Der Logos und sein Prophet', in *Apophoreta*, BZNW 30, 1964, 109–34: '. . . that I would like to see stronger stress on the connection between the prologue and Alexandrian Judaism. This happened in earlier scholarship before Bultmann. I think that gnostic connections were only communicated by means of Hellenistic Jewish literature, of which no more than a fragment has been preserved' (122, n. 30). 'Gnostic connections' can be completely ignored in the prologue; Jewish Hellenistic thought, which we may picture as having been extremely varied, is a quite adequate explanation.

'Christ is the end of the law, that everyone who has faith may be justified' (Rom. 10.4) is a fundamental expression of the unique soteriological function of the crucified and exalted Jesus as the all-embracing, final, eschatological revelation of God which challenges the claim of the law in principle. It is not just Moses, but God's Christ alone, who brings salvation. Paul's appeal to the Corinthians, 'God made Christ Jesus our wisdom, our righteousness and sanctification and redemption' (I Cor. 1.30), in essentials embraces all the functions of salvation which the pious Jews ascribed to Wisdom-Torah. Behind this break stood an inexorably consistent piece of christological thinking. It must have been a fatal scandal to his Jewish contemporaries for God's Wisdom no longer to be communicated by the venerable body of law which Moses received on Sinai but by a seducer of the people who was broken on the cross.[131] We cannot therefore over-exaggerate the scandal of Pauline christology and soteriology, precisely *because* it was fed from Jewish sources. Of course this scandal was not so much grounded in the teaching of the pre-existent Son of God, as H. J. Schoeps believed, but in the christologically motivated abrogation of the law, its abolition as a way of salvation by the cross and resurrection of Jesus.

The connection between Jesus and Wisdom had thus been prepared for by Jesus' own preaching during his ministry, the form of which was very much in the wisdom tradition. The primitive Palestine community collected the unique wisdom teachings of the Messiah in the nucleus of the logia source, just as earlier the wise sayings of King Solomon, David's son, had also been collected together. Of course, in the case of Jesus, 'more than Solomon is here' (Luke 11.31 = Matt. 12.42). He was seen already as the representative of divine Wisdom, and the features of Wisdom which we also find in the case of the Son of Man in the Jewish

---

[131] For Jesus' opponents, the high-priestly Sadducees and the Pharisees who were faithful to the Torah, Jesus was not only a figure who had met with human failure, but a perverter of the people who had been judged by God: see M. Hengel, *Nachfolge und Charisma*, 43ff. The contrast between his claim and his shameful death had to be interpreted as the divine judgment. That is why Paul, the Pharisee and zealot for the law, became a persecutor of the community.

Similitudes of Ethiopian Enoch were transferred to him.[132] Here is another confirmation that the development of christology was from the beginning concerned with synthesis: otherwise it was impossible to give satisfactory expression to the eschatological uniqueness of God's communication of himself in the man Jesus. Not only mediation at creation but also the designation of Christ as 'God's image' (εἰκών) was taken over from the wisdom tradition of Greek-speaking Judaism. At the same time, this concept created associations between the pre-existent Christ and the figure of the first, heavenly Adam, the 'primal man', who in Philo is identical with the Logos and the 'firstborn son', though it is striking that Paul does not see Christ as the protological primal man of Gen. 1 and 2, but as the heavenly, eschatological Adam, who as a 'life-giving spirit' overcomes death.[133] The 'first Adam', the

[132] F. Christ, *Jesus Sophia. Die Sophia-Christologie bei den Synoptikern*, ATANT 57, 1970; H. Koester/J. M. Robinson, *Trajectories through Early Christianity*, 1971, 71ff., 179ff., 219ff. For the unique words of the Messiah see M. Hengel, *TQ* 153, 1973, 267, n. 42: Ps. Sol. 17.43; T. Levi 18.1; Targ. Isa. 53.5, 11, cf. Luke 4.16ff. Here I follow F. Mussner, *Galaterbrief*, 86, n. 43, in believing that there is no 'existence of a special "Q group" ' among the early Christian communities, with a quite specific, distinctive theology without a kerygma of the cross and resurrection. Still less are these, as S. Schulz asserts, sayings of the exalted Jesus. There is no mention of the exalted Christ in Q, which with few exceptions is concerned throughout with the words of the earthly Jesus. As the spirit was regularly present in Christian prophets in the liturgy, there was no need to record and hand down what he had made known; what was important was the teaching of the earthly Jesus, who had now been removed from the community, and this was seen as the apocalyptic wisdom-teaching of the Messiah. The reason why there is no kerygma of the passion and the resurrection is that this was not part of the proclamation of Jesus. The best solution to the riddle of Q is to take Q seriously as a record of the teaching of Jesus. The basic theory of S. Schulz, *Q. Die Spruchquelle der Evangelisten*, 1972, 5, is that 'Earliest Christianity, long (!) before Paul wrote his letter, . . . was from the beginning a complex entity with a variety of traditional material and different outlines of the kerygma, which indicate different independent communities.' In this form it is untenable and misleading.

[133] For Christ as the 'image of God', II Cor. 4.4; Col. 1.15; cf. J. Jervell, *Imago Dei*, FRLANT 76, 1960, 173ff., 197ff., and especially 227ff., on the 'divine status of Christ'; F.-W. Eltester, *Eikon im Neuen Testament*, BZNW 23, 1958, 130ff. For Adam and Christ see I Cor. 15.44-49. Here Paul breaks through the protological speculation of the diaspora synagogue

primal man, does not have any function as eschatological redeemer in Judaism, either. Now if Christ is identical with the heavenly, *pre-temporal* 'image of God', that also means that he was '*of divine nature*', as we hear at the beginning of the Philippians hymn. Thus, although he is clearly subordinate, the Son no longer stood on the side of creation alone, but also on the side of God. Only through the incarnation, which is 'consummated' in his death on the cross, does he receive a share in human destiny and can he be regarded as reconciler and intercessor for men. Jesus was now no longer just the perfect righteous man, chosen by God, who was in complete accord with God's will, a model for discipleship, but in addition the divine mediator who out of the Father's love for lost men obediently gave up his heavenly communion with the Father and took on human form and human destiny, a destiny which led to a shameful death on the cross. Thus incarnation and death become an unsurpassable expression of the divine love. Neither Graeco-Roman nor Jewish tradition knew of such a 'myth'. In the Son, God himself came to men and was involved with their deepest distress, therein to reveal his love to all creatures. Only as the broken figure on the cross was Jesus – paradoxically – the exalted one, the Lord, to whom, as God's eschatological 'plenipotentiary', were subjected even those powers which had apparently triumphed over him at his ignominious death (Phil. 2.6–11; I Cor. 2.8; II Cor. 8.9). It is understandable that bold christological sketches of this kind were not at first presented in the form of speculative prose, but in hymns inspired by the spirit (I Cor. 14.26; cf. Col. 3.16; Eph. 5.19; Rev. 5.9, etc.); the language most appropriate to God's 'inexpressible grace' (II Cor. 9.15) was the hymn of praise inspired by the Spirit. The quotation of such a hymn in teaching or paraenesis shows that it quickly acquired 'the status of a sacred text' in the same way as Old Testament statements.[134]

---

with his very specific eschatology. There is no longer any need to look for a gnostic background. On the other hand, the apocalyptic Son of Man could very well underlie the 'last Adam' of I Cor. 15.45. For Jewish speculation about Adam see J. E. Ménard, *RSR* 42, 1968, 291f.

[134] R. Deichgräber, *Gotteshymnus und Christushymnus in der frühen Christenheit*, SUNT 5, 1967, 188f.

IV. *Kyrios and Son of God*

This development in christology progressed *in a very short time*. Its final result was that the statements in the Old Testament in which the inexpressible divine name, the tetragrammaton YHWH or its Qere in the Greek Bible, Kyrios, 'Lord', was used, were now transferred directly to the *Kyrios Jesus*. Paul can already give Joel 3.5, 'Everyone who calls upon the name of the Lord will be saved' (Rom. 10.13; cf. Acts 2.21), as the basis for the key acclamation 'Κύριος Ἰησοῦς'. In the original text, Kyrios refers to God himself, but for Paul the Kyrios is Jesus, in whom God makes a full disclosure of his salvation. From the time of the history of religions school there has been an inclination to derive this terminology from the mystery cults with their 'Kyria Isis' or 'Kyrios Sarapis', but this is a quite senseless undertaking.[135] Quite apart from the

[135] This old theory of W. Bousset and W. Heitmüller has enjoyed great popularity down to quite recent times, see S. Schulz, 'Maranatha und Kyrios Jesus', *ZNW* 53, 1962, 125–44; W. Kramer, *Christ, Lord, Son of God*, SBT 50, 1966, 96ff.; P. Vielhauer, *Aufsätze zum NT*, ThB 31, 1965, 166, in a quite irrelevant, one might almost say 'scholastic', piece of polemic against F. Hahn, *Christologische Hoheitstitel*, FRLANT 83, 1963, 67–125. Whereas Hahn for the most part gives a convincing account of the historical situation, Vielhauer is still completely oriented on the old and unexamined theories of the history of religions school; similarly K. Wengst, *Christologische Formeln und Lieder des Urchristentums*, SNT 7, 1972, 131ff. To assert that the title Kyrios was 'a general predicate of gods in Hellenistic cults . . . above all in the mysteries' (134) is facile and simply misleading. Where and from what point are the gods of Eleusis and Dionysus, the real mystery gods, 'generally' given the title 'Kyrios'? Since when has it been possible to demonstrate that Attis and Mithras were 'mystery gods' (see above, pp. 25ff., n. 54)? From what point and whereabouts in Syria (which is the important question for us) do they appear, along with the title Kyrios? One exception is the 'Kyria Isis' from the first century BC. Possibly in her case – and in the case of Sarapis, as H. Stegermann conjectures in his work on the title Kyrios, which unfortunately has yet to be published – there is a reaction against the usurping of the title Kyrios by the Jews, who used the word 'Lord' as Qere for the tetragrammaton. (In Egypt they were numerous and influential.) To use 'Kyrios' in the absolute as a divine title is essentially un-Greek. We find the designation 'Lord' that much more frequently in a variety of forms in connection with Semitic deities in Syria, Palestine and Mesopotamia, the Jews not excepted. Thus 'Kyrios' appears quite often as a title for local Baalim who were accorded the functions of Zeus, or even for Egyptian

fact that Sarapis only became a mystery god at a late date and then remained on the fringe of the mysteries,[136] the title 'Kyrios' is not typical of the mysteries. Moreover, we have no evidence for mysteries in Syria in the first century BC (see pp. 27ff., above). The

deities in the later period. The title expresses a personal relationship with the deity, which was so important for the oriental. Angels, too, could be addressed as 'Kyrios' and were called 'kyrioi'. For 'Lord' was not only a divine title or mode of address, but also the title for all kinds of distinguished people, including the Herodian kings and not least the emperor after the time of Claudius. Finally, it is striking that the Greek title 'Kyrios' is very rarely used of gods even in the Syrian inscriptions before the second century AD. This whole question calls for a thorough investigation, which I hope to make in due course. The critical observation made by K. Berger, *NTS* 17, 1970/71, 413, is quite correct: 'The claim, however, persists. It is quite mysterious how it could have been possible in terms of the history of the tradition for Jesus to be identified with a Hellenistic cult deity. The theory that Gentile Christians alone were responsible for this transference is untenable, because there is early evidence for the title, and "pure" Gentile Christianity is a fiction.' I can therefore only agree with Vielhauer's polemical remark, 'Problems are not solved by ignoring them' (166). The only question is who has so far ignored the decisive problem, namely what the sources say! For this whole question see also M. Hengel, in *Neues Testament und Geschichte, Festschrift O. Cullmann*, 1972, 55ff., and above all W. Foerster, *Herr ist Jesus*, 1924, with its excellent collections of material. See especially 79ff. on the mystery cults: 'Popular religion formed the basis for the later mysteries. Where *kyrios* had not already been used, it did not appear in the mysteries, either with Attis or with Mithras. The Isis mysteries indicate that even where *kyrios* was a customary usage, it was used less often in the mysteries. The corresponding term there is ἄνασσα, queen, which means "ruler" ' (89). Foerster's conclusions are largely confirmed by more recent material, see the continuation of his work in *TDNT* 3, 1039–58.

[136] A. D. Nock, *Essays*, 2, 799: 'Apart from one possible exception in a papyrus, there is no other indication of any mysteries of Sarapis himself.' See the verdict of the best authority, P. M. Fraser, *Ptolemaic Alexandria*, 1972, 1, 265, and 2, 419, n. 20. It is probable that the papyrus mentioned by Nock (PSI 1162, third century AD) also contains no reference to the mysteries. See id., *Opuscula Atheniensia* 3, 1969, 4, n. 1. It should also be noted that the new god created by Ptolemy I in the early empire was markedly less significant outside Egypt. This significance only increased as a result of Vespasian's enthronement in Alexandria in 69 BC and then again through Hadrian. The god reached his greatest period as universal god in the third century AD. The very isolated references to Sarapis mysteries are late and their meaning is disputed. Presumably he only became a mystery god occasionally through his identification with Osiris

and in conjunction with the Isis mysteries, for which there is similarly evidence after the first century AD. See L. Vidman, *Isis und Sarapis bei den Griechen und Römern*, RVV 29, 1970, 126ff., and id., *Sylloge inscriptionum religionis Isiacae et Sarapiacae*, RVV 28, 1969, no. 758 = CIL II, 2395c from Portugal, third century AD. No. 326, second century AD Prusa, and no. 295, Tralles, are uncertain. That the Eumolpid Timotheus of Eleusis was involved in the foundation of the cult (Tacitus, *Hist.* 4, 83, and Plutarch, *Is. et Osir.* 28, 362A) is still no proof that it had the character of a mystery. Neither the number of places where the mysteries of Isis (and Osiris) could be performed nor the number of initiates should be over-estimated. These were 'exclusive clubs', 'as the mysteries in all the oriental mystery religions in imperial times were very expensive' (Vidman, *Isis und Sarapis*, 127). The kind of 'solemn initiation' which Apuleius describes, e.g. at Cenchraea and Rome, 'could only take place where there was a well-appointed temple with a number of priests who also acted in these mystic games' (op. cit., 131). Nor is it a coincidence that both Sarapis inscriptions and archaeological evidence for Syria, Phoenicia and Palestine are relatively rare. See Vidman, *Sylloge*, 180ff., and G. J. F. Kater-Sibbes, *Preliminary Catalogue of Sarapis Monuments*, 1973, 76ff. The same holds for the Isis cult, see F. Dunand, *Le culte d'Isis dans le bassin oriental*, 1973, 3, 122ff.: with very few exceptions, the spread of the cults of Isis and Sarapis in Syria can be demonstrated only in the time of the empire: 'En Palestine, que ce soit sur le littoral ou à l'intérieur du pays, les traces du culte isiaque sont très rares' (132). The situation in Rome and Italy is different, see M. Malaise, *Les conditions de pénétration et de diffusion des cultes égyptiens en Italie*, 1972. Here too, however, intensive expansion only begins with the Flavians (407ff.). The few Isis inscriptions from Syria and Palestine, see L. Vidman, *Sylloge inscriptionum religionis Isiacae et Sarapiacae*, 1969, 181–6, contain no references to mysteries: *kyrios/kyria* appears only in an Artemis inscription, three or four times for the emperor and twice for the city goddess of Gerasa (κυρία πατρίς), i.e. *not* for the mystery gods. The reason why Sarapis sometimes attracted the title Kyrios is that, like Asclepius, as a god connected with salvation, dreams and oracles, he had a personal relationship to believers. This was similarly the case with Kyrios in the Christian community right from the beginning. It means, however, that personal relationship with the exalted Christ cannot first have been established in alien pagan cults. That the 'Lord Jesus' *could* be seen as a kind of new cult-deity at a later stage in typically Hellenistic mission communities of an almost exclusively Gentile-Christian stamp is another chapter in the story. It was possible, for example, in Corinth, and then led to corresponding misunderstandings among certain groups, but it was certainly not yet the case for the 'pre-Pauline' and 'early Pauline' mission. These groups hardly exercised any theological influence in the early period. The element coming from the Jewish Christians or the God-fearers was simply too strong for this. For the problem see already J. Weiss, *Earliest Christianity*, 1937 reprinted 1959, 31ff., 161f., 172f., 233f.

development from 'rabbi' or 'mari', used as a respectful form of address to Jesus, to the fully developed Kyrios can be shown to have as stringent an intrinsic consistency as the development in the use of the term Son of God.[137] Here Ps. 110.1, the most important Old Testament proof passage for the development of christology, acquired a quite decisive role.[138] Philo, too, can say in *Somn.* 1, 157 that Jacob saw the *Kyrios* on the heavenly ladder in his dream (Gen. 28.13), meaning by it the 'archangel', i.e. the Logos, in whose form God reveals himself. Here he distinguishes between a proper mention of ὁ θεός and an improper mention with the mere θεός, which means 'his eldest Logos' as mediator of revelation (1, 228–230).

Finally, I would like to call attention to just one more example which shows that even in Palestine itself, the Essenes of Qumran in their eschatological exegesis could transfer Old Testament passages, the original text of which clearly meant God himself, to a mediator or redeemer figure near to God. This is the well-known fragment from Cave 11 in which the prince of light and adversary of darkness, Michael-Melchizedek, appears as eschatological victor over all the powers of evil and ushers in the eschatological year of jubilee (according to Lev. 25.8), which is identical with the proclamation of liberation in Isa. 61.1 (cf. Luke 4.17ff.).[139] The first

---

[137] F. Hahn, *Christologische Hoheitstitel*, 74ff.; M. Hengel, *Nachfolge und Charisma*, 46ff., cf. above, p. 46, n. 92: Metatron's name too 'is like that of his Lord'. According to Philo, the name Kyrios embodies a special *dynamis* of God. Cf. now J. A. Fitzmyer, n. 89 above, 386ff.

[138] See already H. Windisch, against W. Heitmüller and W. Bousset, in *Neutestamentliche Studien, Festschrift G. Heinrici zum 70. Geburtstag*, 1914, 229, n. 1: 'Furthermore, Ps. 110 should also be taken into account as the biblical basis for the earliest Christian and Pauline doctrine of the heavenly Kyrios and for its origin and development.' Windisch conjectures that Ps. 110.3 prompted Paul to fuse the idea of the Messiah with Wisdom in Prov. 8.22. Presumably this step was already taken in the Greek-speaking Jewish-Christian community which existed before, or better alongside, Paul. The later rabbinic application of Ps. 110 to Abraham was virtually a last resort.

[139] A. S. v. d. Woude, 'Melchisedek als himmlische Erlösergestalt in den neugefundenen eschatologischen Midraschim aus Qumran Höhle XI', *OTS* 14, 1965, 354–73; M. de Jonge/A. S. v. d. Woude, *NTS* 12, 1965–66, 301–26; J. A. Fitzmyer, *JBL* 86, 1967, 25–41 = *Essays on the Semitic*

thing which is striking here is that this supreme angelic figure in Qumran is evidently identified with the priest-king Melchizedek of Salem according to Gen. 14.18ff., i.e. an originally human form. It is therefore no coincidence that in Hebrews Melchizedek becomes the type of Christ, the heavenly high priest. In this fragment, Ps. 82.1, 'God has taken his place in the divine council; in the midst of the gods he holds judgment', is interpreted in terms of the eschatological judgment of Michael-Melchizedek on the angels who are hostile to God. It is still more remarkable that the confession of the messenger of peace in Isa. 52.7, 'who says to Zion, "Your God is king" ', does not apply to God himself but again to his plenipotentiary Melchizedek-Michael. The kingdom of God is identical with that of his vizir. According to the most recent reconstruction by Milik, the text says, 'and "your God", that means (Melchizedek, who will deliver) them (from) the hand of Belial'.[140] God's plenipotentiary Michael-Melchizedek, the prince or angel of light, is at the same time the victorious eschatological counterpart of Belial, the 'prince of darkness', who in a new text is called *malki-resa*[c] and appears along with the thrice-named prince of light, *malki-zedeq*, in a vision of Amram, the father of Moses.[141] This unique significance of Michael-Melchizedek among the Jewish Hasidim of the Maccabean period and later among the Essenes of Qumran is confirmed by his role as eschatological mediator of salvation in Dan. 12.1f., where Michael, 'the great prince', emerges as Israel's ally and ushers in the last events. He also appears in the Apocalypse of the Symbolic Animals (Eth. Enoch 90.14, 17, 20ff.), which comes from the same time, and above all the War Scroll, where God sends Michael as 'heavenly redeemer':

Background of the New Testament, 1971, 245–67. There is now a fundamental study by J. T. Milik, 'Milkî-ṣedeq et Milkî-rešaᶜ dans les anciens écrits juifs et chrétiens', *JJS* 23, 1972, 95–144. Cf. also F. du Toit Laubscher, *JSJ* 3, 1972, 46–51.

[140] See the text in Milik, op. cit., 98f., lines 10, 23–25.

[141] J. T. Milik, '4Q Visions de 'Amram et une citation d'Origène', *RB* 79, 1972, 77–79. Both 'Malki-rešaᶜ' and 'Malki-ṣedeq' 'have power over all the sons of Adam', Fr. 1, line 12 (p. 79). One 'rules over all darkness' and the other 'over all light and over all (that belongs to God)', Fr. 2, lines 5f. Cf. also the already-known text 1QS 3. 18ff.

And he will send eternal succour to the company of his (re)deemed
by the might of the angel of the powerful one(?)[142] for the kingdom
of Michael in eternal light; to enlighten with joy the covenant of
Israel . . .; *to raise up among the gods* (*'elim* = angels) *the kingdom of
Michael and the kingdom of Israel above all flesh* (1 QM 17, 6–8).[143]

One could also refer to the Old Slavonic book of Enoch, where
Melchizedek – apparently the great-grandson of Enoch and the
nephew of Noah – is begotten and born in miraculous fashion,
appointed priest and transported by Michael into the garden of
Eden, an indication that that idea of the virgin birth was not completely alien at least to Greek-speaking Judaism.[144] Philo, on the
other hand, interprets the priest-king from Salem of Gen. 14.18f.
as 'the priestly Logos' (*Leg. all.*, 3, 82). The patristic interpretation
of Melchizedek as an angel may also go back to Jewish traditions.
Even the gnostic Melchizedekians who are described by Hippo-

[142] The *ml'k h'dyr'* can be translated in three different ways: see the
commentary by J. v. d. Ploeg, *Le rouleau de la Guerre*, 1959, 177. With
A. S. v. d. Woude, I read *hā'addīr* in the sense of a construct. The 'mighty
one' would then be God. Another possibility is to take *h'dyr* as hiphil with
the following *lmšrt myk'l*: 'he glorifies the rule of Michael'. It seems to me
less probable that it should be interpreted as an adjective with the preced-
ing noun without an article, as this is first attested in Mishnaic Hebrew.

[143] 1QM 17, 6f. For the part played by Michael in Qumran see Y. Yadin,
The Scroll of the War of the Sons of Light against the Sons of Darkness,
1962, 134ff.; O. Betz, *Der Paraklet*, AGSU 2, 1963, 64ff., 149ff., who also
draws attention to the relationships with christology and especially to the
Paraclete in John. The *hārim* corresponds to the New Testament (ὑπερ)-
υψοῦν, cf. Phil. 2.9. For the interpretation of the heavenly mediator and
redeemer figure Melchizedek-Michael see J. T. Milik, *JJS* 23, 1972, 125:
'Milkî-ṣedeq est par conséquent quelque chose de plus qu'un ange créé,
ou même le chef des bons esprits, identifiable à Michaël (comme le
soulignent à juste titre les éditeurs hollandais). Il est en réalité une hypo-
stase de Dieu, autrement dit le Dieu transcendant lorsqu'il agit dans le
monde, Dieu lui-même sous la forme visible où il apparaît aux hommes,
et non pas un ange créé distinct de Dieu (Ex. 23, 20).' There are interesting connections with Philo here. In *De agr.* 51, Philo interprets Ex. 23.20
in terms of God's *'true reason, the firstborn Son'* (τὸν ὀρθὸν αὐτοῦ λόγον
καὶ πρωτόγονον υἱόν) who is appointed by God like a 'governor of the
Great King' to rule the world; cf. also *Migr. Abr.* 174.

[144] A. Vaillant, *Le livre des secrets d'Hénoch. Texte slave et traduction
française*, 1951, 69ff. (chs. 22f.). The narrative displays no Christian
features. It is also improbable that the virgin birth would be ascribed by a
Christian to an Old Testament figure.

lytus and Epiphanius hardly developed out of the exegesis of the Epistle to the Hebrews, and may also have Jewish roots. Among other things, they asserted that 'Melchizedek is greater than Christ, and Christ is only his image' (Hippolytus, *Phil.* 7, 36). Anti-Christian and anti-gnostic polemic is the reason why the rabbis partially devalued the figure of Melchizedek and no longer interpreted Ps. 110. 1, 4 in terms of the Messiah but in terms of Abraham. Thus there was probably a preparation for the typological relationship between the Son of God and the priest-king in *Hebrews* in the Haggadic exegesis of the various Jewish groups.[145]

[145] Cf. G. Wuttke, *Melchisedech der Priesterkönig von Salem*, BZNW 5, 1927, 18ff., 27ff.; G. Bardy, 'Melchisédech dans la tradition patristique', *RB* 35, 1926, 496ff.; 36, 1927, 25ff.; J. A. Fitzmyer, *Essays on the Semitic Background of the New Testament*, 1971, 221ff. 245ff.; cf. M. de Jonge and A. S. v.d. Woude, '11Q Melchizedek and the New Testament', *NTS* 12, 1965/66, 301ff.; O. Michel, *Der Brief an die Hebräer*, KEK ¹²1966, 257ff.

7

The Son in the Epistle
to the Hebrews:
The Crucified and Exalted Jesus

A not unimportant difference between the New Testament and the majority of Jewish texts is of course that New Testament christology *a priori* put the exalted Jesus, as Son, *above all angelic beings* (not least because of his close association with the pre-existent wisdom of God). A real *angel christology* could only become significant right on the fringe of the Jewish-Christian sphere. Jewish angelology is, in fact, already substantially transcended in the Melchizedek text from Qumran. At any rate, in his great work *The Formation of Christian Dogma*, Martin Werner much exaggerated the role of 'angel christology' in early Christianity.[146]

[146] M. Werner, *Die Enstehung des christlichen Dogmas*, [1]1941; [2]1953, 302ff. (an abridged translation appeared in English, *The Formation of Christian Dogma*, [2]1957, 120ff.); this was already questioned by W. Michaelis, *Zur Engelchristologie im Urchristentum*, ATANT 1, 1942. See also J. Barbel, *Christos Angelos*, Bonn dissertation 1941; H.-J. Schoeps, *Theologie und Geschichte des Judenchristentums*, 1949, 8off.; R. N. Longenecker, 'Early Christological Motifs', *NTS* 14, 1967–68, 528ff. The penetration of certain themes of 'angel christology' in the 'post-apostolic' period, e.g. in the Shepherd of Hermas, is closely connected with the collapse of theological reflection generally. Cf. e.g. L. Pernveden, *The Concept of the Church in the Shepherd of Hermas*, Stud. Theol. Lund 27, 1966, 58ff., 'The Son of God and Michael'. In certain areas where there was a pre-Christian angel cult under Jewish influence, e.g. in Phrygia, people were particularly open to 'angel syncretism', as Colossians shows. Cf. L. Robert, *Hellenica* 10, 434, n. 2, and CRAI, 1971 613f. The constant influence of Jewish apocrypha, with speculations about angels and hypostases, on early Christian popular piety, must also be taken into account, see e.g. C. Colpe, *JbAC* 15, 1972, 8ff., on the Apocryphon of Peter from Codex VI of Nag Hammadi, where Jesus appears to the

The Epistle to the Hebrews follows earlier Christian tradition closely in making a fundamental distinction between the pre-existent and exalted Son and the angels, and in putting the Son far above the angels by virtue of his association with the Father:

> He reflects the glory of God (cf. Wisd. 7.25f.)
> and bears the very stamp of his nature,
> upholding the universe by his word of power.
> When he had made purification for sins,
> he sat down at the right hand of the Majesty on high,
> having become as much superior to the angels
> as the name he has obtained is more excellent than theirs.
> For to what angel did (God) say at any time,
> 'Thou art my Son, today I have begotten thee'?
> Or again, 'I will be to him a father, and he shall be to me a son'?
> And again, when he brings the firstborn into the world, he says,
> 'Let all God's angels worship him.'[147]

In this context we should note that Judaism was also familiar with the theme of the jealousy of angels, who were given a lower status

---

disciples in the form of a healing angel, Lithargoel. The 'ancestral angelic folklore' of Jewish-Christian circles could now live on 'as angel christology' (op. cit., 10f.). Traces of this can be followed as far as Origen. However, in contrast to the colourful world of images in Jewish-Christian angelology, theological reflection followed the course to the divinity of Christ in the unity of the revelation of Father and Son with intrinsic consistency.

[147] Heb. 1.3–6. For the dispute over the christology of Hebrews and its soteriological and anthropological interpretation see E. Grässer, in *Neues Testament und christliche Existenz, Festschrift für Herbert Braun*, 1973, 195–206. For the interpretation of the introductory verses of the epistle see id., EKK 3, 1971, 55–91. For the theme of Christ's superiority to the angels see 1 Clem. 36.2, which in my view already presupposes knowledge of Hebrews. The rather later Shepherd of Hermas shows that the question of the relationship of Christ to the angels was acute in Rome at the end of the first century and the beginning of the second. In contrast to G. Theissen, *Untersuchungen zum Hebräerbrief*, SNT 2, 1969, 120ff., 'gnostic themes' should not be presupposed in Hebrews, much less in Philo, unless the term 'gnostic' is clearly differentiated from later Gnosticism. The abundant use, or better misuse, of the term 'gnostic' only serves to confuse matters. See on the other hand the detailed historical investigation by O. Hofius, *Katapausis*, WUNT 11, 1970, and id., *Der Vorhang vor dem Throne Gottes*, WUNT 14, 1972, who has clearly brought out the many strata in the Jewish background to the letter. These was still no division between an 'orthodox' and a 'heretical' Judaism before AD 70.

than a particularly distinctive man, in the context of the creation of Adam, the bestowing of the law on Israel and the ascension and exaltation of particular figures of salvation history like Enoch-Metatron, Moses, or the martyr high priest Ishmael b. Elisha. According to later rabbinic teaching, the righteous man was 'greater than the angels, for the angels, unlike the righteous man, cannot hear the voice of God without fear. The angel Gabriel followed Daniel and his companions like a pupil going behind his master.'[148] Of course, the primitive Christian exaltation christology left all these intermediary stages behind in a bold move in christological thinking. E. Lohmeyer is quite right in stressing in his interpretation of Heb. 1.1ff. that the essential point here is that the christological outline of Phil. 2.6–11 is being made more precise. Here the 'notion of equality with God is defined (more exactly); the metaphysical determination "Son" frees it from the indefiniteness which the phrase "being in the form of God" still carries with it.' The subjection of 'everything in heaven' to the name of Jesus (Phil. 2.10f.) corresponds to his superiority over the angels (Heb. 1.4). But the 'heir of the universe' (Heb. 1.2, cf. 4b) is the exalted Kyrios. 'Thus the divine nature of the "Son" in Hebrews is so to speak established from the beginning. The approach here is the same as in the hymn which Paul quotes; the difference is that it is made more precise in terms of the metaphysical substantiality of Christ.'[149] The decisive feature here is that a strict paradox is maintained: the humiliation of Jesus to the point of his shameful death on the accursed cross, which was such a scandal for ancient man, whether Jew or Greek (I Cor. 1.18ff.), is sustained in an unbroken and indeed remorseless way. The basic theme of the Epistle to the Hebrews, on which there are many variations, is the representative atoning suffering of the Son. Neither his temptation (2.18) nor his loud cries and tears in prayer (5.7) are suppressed. 'He endured the cross, despising the shame' (12.2). It is no coinci-

[148] R. Mach, *Der Zaddik in Talmud und Midrasch*, 1957, 110; cf. also P. Schäfer, *Rivalität zwischen Engeln und Menschen. Untersuchungen zur rabbinischen Engelvorstellung*, Studia Judaica VIII, 1975.

[149] E. Lohmeyer, *Kyrios Jesus. Eine Untersuchung zu Phil 2,5–11*, reprinted 1961, 77f.

dence that Cicero, in his second speech against Verres (5, 165), speaks of crucifixion as the '*crudelissimum taeterrimum supplicium*'. 'So Jesus also suffered . . . in order to sanctify the people through his own blood. The reforelet us go forth to him outside the camp, bearing his *shame*' (13.12f.).[150] One might almost regard the whole of Hebrews as a large-scale development of the christological theme which is already present in the Philippians hymn. It is remarkable that at the very point where the divine sonship and pre-existence of the exalted Christ are stressed, the shame of his passion also stands in the centre. This is true for Paul, for the author of Hebrews and – in a somewhat different form – for the Second (Mark 15.39) and Fourth Evangelists (John 19.5). The '*doxa*' of the Son of God cannot be separated from the shame of his cross. The Fourth Evangelist gives classic form to this idea: the crucified Jesus is the exalted Christ (3.14; 8.28). Conversely, it is probably no chance that the Hellenist Luke keeps his distance from both the christology of the pre-existent Son of God and the saving significance of the cross. The tense christological struggle in the ancient church could never completely free itself from this paradoxical dialectic. The Scythian monks in Constantinople were still fighting over the recognition of the disputed 'theopaschite formula': *unus ex trinitate passus est carne*, in the sixth century AD. For traditional Greek ideas of God oriented on Parmenides' way of thinking, the idea of the suffering of the pre-existent Son of God was and remained an intolerable scandal. The 'theologically progressive' intellectuals of the second century AD therefore fled from this intolerable paradox of the christological confession into gnostic docetism. Here was one of the chief reasons for the success of the gnostic type of thinking in the church of the second and third centuries AD.

---

[150] See my forthcoming study, 'Mors turpissima crucis', in *Rechtfertigung. Festschrift für E. Käsemann zum 70. Geburtstag*, 1976, und 'Die christologischen Hoheitstitel im Urchristentum', in *Der Name Gottes*, ed. H. V. Stietencron, 1975, 90–111.

8

Theological Conclusions

With this glance forward we have gone far beyond the horizon of our investigation, which has been no more than an attempt to understand better the christological development of the first twenty dark years between about AD 30 and AD 50, by means of the title Son of God, at the same time casting light on its historical background. In so doing we came up against a multiplicity of Jewish ideas about a mediator and redeemer, from Enoch-Metatron through Wisdom and the Logos to Melchizedek-Michael. We discovered not only analogies but also fundamental differences. A demonstration of parallels in the history of religions always sharpens one's awareness of the difference and the new elements which came out in primitive Christianity. Precisely in order to express the uniqueness of the revelation of the *one* God in a hostile world and his history with the chosen people Israel, ancient Judaism was able to make use of many different conceptions of intermediaries. These intermediary figures were differentiated from God and yet closely connected with him. They acquired special significance in the final eschatological events. It is understandable that post-Christian Judaism partly retracted these forms of expression: polemical differentiation from Christian and gnostic 'heretics' made rethinking necessary. However, Jewish mysticism shows that even at a later time it was felt undesirable and impossible to give them up altogether. Investigation of the significance of the Jewish Hekalot and Merkabah literature for early Christian christology has still a wide field to explore, as Billerbeck in his great commentary unfortunately paid too little attention to these texts, Odeberg's exegesis of the Gospel of John has remained a torso and Jewish scholars have often underestimated the significance of them, for apologetic reasons.[151]

[151] The two works by O. Hofius cited in n. 147 are an excellent example

These forms of Jewish thought and language concerned with a mediator of revelation and salvation at the beginning and the end of time almost forced earliest Christianity to interpret Jesus' preaching and actions, his claim to be God's eschatological messianic ambassador, his unique connection with the Father, the imminence of whose salvation he announced, his shameful death and his resurrection, which was interpreted as exaltation, in a concentrated form as a *unique*, '*eschatological*' *saving event*. The general apocalyptic framework of earliest Christianity, in which the revelation of the 'saving power' of God through this Jesus was expressed, from the beginning irresistibly forced the development of christological thought in this direction. The goal was to articulate God's communication of himself, his speaking and acting in the Messiah Jesus, in quite unsurpassable, final – 'eschatological' – form. The roots of this development were twofold: first, Jesus' claim to messianic authority, in which he announced the imminence of the rule of God, i.e. the saving love of the Father, to the lost, and secondly the disciples' certainty that God had raised his crucified Messiah Jesus. It was impossible to stop at a simple adoptionist christology or an understanding of Jesus as a new lawgiver, because this would have continued to give God's action in creation and in primal times, as with his people Israel under the old covenant, an independence from his conclusive, eschatological revelation in Jesus, which was open to misinterpretation. With strictly consistent christological thought, the early communities were concerned with the *whole revelation of God*, the *whole of salvation* in his Christ Jesus, which could not remain one 'episode in salvation history' among others. In Jesus, God himself comes to men with the fullness of his love. It was through a christology in terms of the pre-existent Son of God, which was apparently so scandalous and, according to a widespread opinion, 'mythological',

---

of the way in which these texts can be used to illuminate the New Testament. The two texts published by J. Strugnell, 'The Angelic Liturgy at Qumran . . .', *Congress Volume Oxford* 1959, SVT 7, 1960, show that we may already presuppose the heavenly Merkabah speculation in pre-Christian times. Unfortunately the great work by G. Scholem is still used too little for New Testament exegesis.

that the way was shown towards overcoming the danger of a syncretistic, mythical speculation. It is no coincidence that the most fully developed christology of the Gospel of John has particularly attracted thinkers like Schleiermacher and Bultmann who have been so strictly concerned with 'demythologizing'.

In a concern to express the revelation of the love of God in this Jesus, for which no reasons could be given from the human side, in such a way that it could be proclaimed as a missionary message, a 'gospel' to 'Jews and Greeks', the earliest Christian community created with astonishing speed a christology in which he appeared as the fulfiller of the promises of the old covenant, the sole mediator of salvation, indeed as the one fulfiller of God's revelation from the beginning. Far from opening the floodgates to mythologizing, to raise him to be Son of God and Lord *above* all heavenly powers and to set him 'at the right hand of the Father' restricted this possibility. This is demonstrated by the course of later gnosticism, where in an abundance of mythological speculations Christ was often degraded to becoming *one* divine emanation *among many others*. Nor was the scandal of the cross removed by this christological development; rather, as far as ancient man was concerned, it was immeasurably increased. There may have been many crucified righteous men in the ancient world: Plato's paradigm in *Republic* 361E was well-known to the educated men of the time. But for Jews and Greeks the crucified Son of God was an unheard-of idea.[152] The danger of ditheism was also averted, for the Son was

[152] Hegesippus in Eusebius, *HE* 2, 23, 12: ὁ λαὸς πλανᾶται ὀπίσω Ἰησοῦ τοῦ σταυρωθέντος, and the objections of the Jew Trypho in Justin, *Dialogue* 10.3: 'But we cannot understand ... how you can set your hopes on a crucified man (cf. 8.3) and expect good of him, although you do not observe God's commandments.' 90.1: 'However, you must prove to us whether he had to be crucified and die such a shameful and dishonourable death, which is accursed by the law, since something like this is unthinkable to us'; see also 137, 1ff. and the *Altercatio Simonis Judaei et Theophili Christiani*, 2, 4, ed. Harnack, TU 1, 1883, 28f., and E. Bratke, CSEL 45, 25f., and E. Bammel, *VigChr* 26, 1972, 259ff., with a text from the *Toledoth Jesu*. From the Hellenistic world see Lucian's taunt about the 'crucified sophist' and his worshippers, *Peregr.* 13, and 11; also the charges of Celsus, Origen, *C. Celsum* 2,9, and the well-known taunt crucifix on the Palatine. W. Bauer, *Das Leben Jesu im Zeitalter der neutestamentlichen Apokryphen*, 1909 reprinted 1967, 467ff., gives a survey

involved in a complete union of action and love with the Father
(John 3.35; 8.19, 28, 40; 15.15; cf. 1.18; 10.30; 17.11, 21–26) to
whom he ultimately hands all things over in complete obedience
(I Cor. 15.28). For that very reason he could not become the symbol of man's self-redemption. Modern dogmatic theologians are
fond of contrasting christologies 'from above' and 'from below',
but this is a false alternative that goes against the course of New
Testament christology, which develops in an indissoluble dialectic
between God's saving activity and man's answer. God's Yes,
which precedes all human action, stands not only at the end of this
course (John 1.14; 3.16), but already at its beginning (Luke 4.18 =
Isa. 61.1; Mark 2.17; Matt. 11.19; Luke 9.20). Jesus the Son, in
eternal communion with the Father, was *not* understood by the
community in the way that Ernst Bloch would have us believe, as
the 'Son of Man' who, like a second Prometheus, stormed heaven
for himself and thus won divine worth for humanity. The Son who
was sent into the world and obediently took upon himself human
existence 'under the law' (Gal. 4.4), and indeed a slave's death, was
not regarded as a religious hero like Heracles, who put human
achievement on a new level. These objectifications, which are all
too familiar from Christian tradition and all too alien to outsiders
because of the extreme 'mythological' form of their expression,
may now seem odd or even scandalous to us. But we should not
allow ourselves to be discouraged from attempting to understand
them better. The disqualification of expressions of this kind, which
often seems scientific but is really only a matter of primitive
'demythologizing', can sometimes also be a sign of spiritual
naïvety and convenience. In reality, theology will never be able to
dispense with the language of 'myth', with its transcendent meta-
phors, and at this very point we would do well to learn from the
example of the greatest Greek 'theologian', Plato. The 'Son of
God' has become an established, unalienable metaphor[153] of

of Jewish and pagan polemic against the crucified Jesus: 'A God or son
of God dying on the cross! That was enough to put an end to the new
religion' (477). See also above 40ff., n. 83; 61ff., n. 113.

[153] See E. Jüngel, 'Metaphorische Wahrheit', in P. Ricoeur/E. Jüngel,
Metapher. Zur Hermeneutik religiöser Sprache, EvTh-Sonderheft, 1974,
71–122; for 'Son of God' especially 71, 73, 111ff., 118.

Christian theology, expressing both the origin of Jesus in God's being (i.e. his love for all creatures and his unique connection with God) and his true humanity.

I am well aware that the interpretation of expressions of Christian faith is the specific and inevitable task of the systematic theologian, but to end with I would like to make some suggestions for any attempt to consider the significance of the New Testament statements about the 'Son of God'.

This phrase is an expression of the following beliefs:

1. God's love towards all men has taken shape in an unsurpassable way, once and for all, in the one man, Jesus of Nazareth, his beloved Son.

2. The event of this love, i.e. our salvation, is not a this-worldly possibility at human disposal but presupposes the sending by the eternal God of Jesus, who is fully 'in accord with' God's being and will.

3. God's words in the Old Testament, i.e. his revelation in creation and in the history of Israel, the chosen people, lead up to his chosen Messiah Jesus and have their consummation in him, 'the Son'.

4. The death of Jesus on the cross and his resurrection represent the bearing of human guilt and man's mortal destiny by God himself, who 'identifies' himself with the man Jesus and in so doing overcomes guilt and death for us all.

5. Belief in God's disclosure of himself in his Son is the basis for the joyful 'freedom of the children of God', a freedom which participates in God's unlimited 'possibility' in this all too limited world and in a future which – thank God! – is not dependent on a humanity which regards itself as the 'supreme being', but belongs wholly and utterly to God's love.

But let Paul have the last word:

'For all who are led by the Spirit of God are sons of God. For you did not receive the spirit of slavery to fall back into fear, but you have received the spirit of sonship. When we cry, "Abba! Father!" it is the Spirit himself bearing witness with our spirit that we are children of God' (Rom. 8.14f.).

Index of Biblical References

Genesis
chs. 1–2 75
1.1 70
1.2 70
1.4 71
5.24 46
6.2, 4 22
14.18ff. 81
18.1ff. 40
18.17 54
18.33 54
22.12, 16 11
28.13 80
32.25ff. 48
42.11 53

Exodus
4.22 48
4.22ff. 22
7.1 42
23.20 82
23.21 47
24.2 55

Leviticus
25.8 80

Numbers
23.19 40

Deuteronomy
13.18 53
14.1 22, 53
21.23 68
32.5 22
32.6 22
32.8f. 22
32.18 22, 53

32.19 22
33.1 55
34.10 69

Joshua
14.6 55

I Samuel
(LXX I Kingdoms)
2.27 55
9.7–10 55

II Samuel
7.12–14 22, 64
7.14 44, 64

I Kings
(LXX III Kingdoms)
12.24 55
13.4–31 55
17.24 55

II Kings
(LXX IV Kingdoms)
1.9–13 55
4.7ff. 55

I Chronicles
17.13 23
22.10 23
28.6 23

Job
1.6 22
2.1 22

Psalms
2 44

2.6 70
2.7 23, 44, 64
8.24 70
29.1 22
82.1 81
82.6 22
89 64
89.4ff. 23
89.7 22
89.27 45
89.28 45, 48
110 62
110.1 80, 83
110.3 23, 69
110.4 83

Proverbs
8.22 70
8.22ff. 49, 51, 70
8.29f. 49

Isaiah
9.5 23
11.2 70, 71
43.6 22
45.11 22
52.7 81
53 64
61.1 80, 92

Jeremiah
3.4 22
31.9 22
31.20 22, 45

Daniel
3.25 22
3.45 13

Index of Modern Authors

100

Peek
Perr
Pesc
Pete
Phil
Plas
Ploe
Pohl
Pöhl
Poko
Pop

Rees
Rein
Reit
Ren
Rico
Riga
Rist
Robe
Robi
Roho
Rolo
Rolo
Rosc
Rose
Rupp

Sand
Sand
Schä
Sche

3, 30, 59, 62